MCWP 4-11.6

I0415706

Petroleum and Water Logistics Operations

U.S. Marine Corps

To Our Readers

Changes: Readers of this publication are encouraged to submit suggestions and changes that will improve it. Recommendations may be sent directly to Commanding General, Marine Corps Combat Development Command, Doctrine Division (C 42), 3300 Russell Road, Suite 318A, Quantico, VA 22134-5021 or by fax to 703-784-2917 (DSN 278-2917) or by E-mail to **nancy.morgan@usmc.mil**. Recommendations should include the following information:

  ı Location of change
       Publication number and title
       Current page number
       Paragraph number (if applicable)
       Line number
       Figure or table number (if applicable)
  ı Nature of change
       Add, delete
       Proposed new text, preferably double-spaced and typewritten
  ı Justification and/or source of change

Additional copies: A printed copy of this publication may be obtained from Marine Corps Logistics Base, Albany, GA 31704-5001, by following the instructions in MCBul 5600, *Marine Corps Doctrinal Publications Status.* An electronic copy may be obtained from the Doctrine Division, MCCDC, world wide web home page which is found at the following universal reference locator: **https://www.doctrine.usmc.mil**.

Unless otherwise stated, whenever the masculine gender is used, both men and women are included.

DEPARTMENT OF THE NAVY
Headquarters United States Marine Corps
Washington, DC 20380-1775

19 June 2005

FOREWORD

Marine Corps Warfighting Publication (MCWP) 4-11.6, *Petroleum and Water Logistics Operations*, provides doctrinal guidance for bulk petroleum and water support of the Marine air-ground task force (MAGTF). This publication is aligned doctrinally with Marine Corps Doctrinal Publication 4, *Logistics*, and tactically with MCWP 4-1, *Logistics Operations*. It specifically addresses the techniques and procedures of bulk fuel and water support of the MAGTF in a joint/multinational environment. MCWP 4-11.6 is a follow-on publication of MCWP 3-17, *Engineer Operations*.

Water and fuel make up the greatest quantities of supply required by the MAGTF to conduct modern warfare. As petroleum or water requirements rise above individual or small unit needs, it becomes necessary to handle them in "bulk" form. Bulk handling calls for special equipment, product handling safeguards, and standing operating procedures. Plant account/permanent facilities are often used at bases, camps, and air stations; however, deploying MAGTFs require special expeditionary systems such as the tactical fuel systems. This publication addresses water and fuel as functional operations. For discussion of water and fuel supply classes, see MCWP 4-11.7, *MAGTF Supply Operations*.

Mission success depends on planning for the known and expecting the unknown. This is especially true when planning bulk liquids operations. Part I discusses bulk fuel operations and part II discusses bulk water operations. Commanders and their staffs at all levels must be concerned about maintaining water and fuel support through completion of the unit's mission. To provide the most effective use of bulk liquids stocks and equipment, bulk liquids planners must be familiar with Marine Corps and Department of Defense bulk liquids assets and responsibilities. To ensure adequate support, commanders and their staffs should address planning for these two commodities in all operation plans.

This publication provides information on the bulk liquids mission, organization, and concept as well as guidance for the planning and conduct of bulk fuel and water support operations for commanders, staffs, subordinate commanders, and personnel in bulk liquid units. Applicable lessons learned have been incorporated in this publication.

This publication supersedes MCWP 4-11.6, *Bulk Liquids Operations*, of 29 August 1996.

Reviewed and approved this date.

BY DIRECTION OF THE COMMANDANT OF THE MARINE CORPS

J. N. MATTIS
Lieutenant General, U.S. Marine Corps
Deputy Commandant for Combat Development

Publication Control Number: 143 000009 00

PETROLEUM AND WATER LOGISTICS OPERATIONS

TABLE OF CONTENTS

Part I. Bulk Fuel Operations 1-1

Chapter 1. Fundamentals. 1-1

Developed Theater 1-1
Undeveloped Theater 1-1
Resupply... 1-1
Marine Corps Forces 1-1
Inland Distribution 1-2

Chapter 2. Organization. 2-1

Organization and Responsibilities 2-1
    Defense Energy Support Center......................... 2-1
    Unified Commands..................................... 2-1
    Joint Bulk Fuel Support 2-1
    Joint Task Force 2-2
Military Services 2-2
    US Army.. 2-2
    US Air Force... 2-2
    US Navy 2-3
    US Marine Corps 2-3

Chapter 3. Tactical Fuel Systems 3-1

Amphibious Assault Fuel System 3-1
Tactical Airfield Fuel Dispensing System 3-3
Helicopter Expedient Refueling System 3-3
Expedient Refueling System 3-3
Six Containers Together................................... 3-3
    Fuel Pump Module..................................... 3-6
    Fuel Tank Modules.................................... 3-6
    Accessories.. 3-6
    Cyclic Resupply 3-6
M970 Mobile Refueler...................................... 3-6
Tactical Petroleum Laboratory, Medium 3-6

USMC Aircraft Bulk Fuel Handling Systems. 3-6
   USMC KC-130R Transport 3-6
   Tactical Bulk Fuel Distribution System 3-7
   Aviation Refueling Capability 3-7
Joint Service Interoperability 3-7
   US Navy Ship-to-Shore Systems 3-7
   US Army Petroleum System. 3-8
   US Air Force Air-based Petroleum System 3-8

Chapter 4. Bulk Fuel Planning **4-1**

Planning Requirements 4-1
   Requirements 4-1
   Sourcing and Procurement 4-1
   Transportation 4-1
   Storage 4-1
   Distribution 4-1
   Equipment 4-2
Planning Considerations 4-2
Planning for Joint Bulk Fuel Operations. 4-2
   Army Petroleum Group. 4-2
   Compatibility 4-2
Marine Corps Bulk Fuel Planning 4-2
   Determine Requirements. 4-3
   Sourcing and Procurement 4-4
   Transportation. 4-4
   Storage 4-4
   Distribution 4-4
War Reserve Requirements and Stocks 4-4
   Petroleum War Reserve Requirement. 4-4
   Petroleum War Reserve Stocks. 4-4
   MEF Petroleum War Reserve Requirement 4-5

Chapter 5. Bulk Fuel Theater Operations **5-1**

Developed Theater 5-1
   Pipeline System. 5-1
   Theater Stockage Objectives. 5-1
Undeveloped Theater 5-1
   Minimum Bulk Fuel Stockage Objective 5-2
   Tactical Hose Line 5-2
   Air Lines of Communications. 5-2
Phases of Bulk Fuel Operations 5-2
   Development. 5-3
   Lodgment 5-3
   Build-up 5-3
Bulk Fuel Operations Within the MAGTF. 5-3
   Command Element 5-3

Combat Service Support Element............................... 5-4
Aviation Combat Element 5-4
Ground Combat Element 5-4
Bulk Fuel Support for the MAGTF 5-5
Resupply.. 5-5
Storage 5-5
Maritime Prepositioning Ships............................... 5-5
Fuel Offload 5-5
Unloading Fuel Systems................................. 5-6
Bulk Fuel Reports... 5-7

Chapter 6. Bulk Fuel Inventory Management....................... 6-1

References.. 6-1
Procedures 6-1
Fuel Accountability 6-2
Reports 6-2

Chapter 7. Bulk Fuel Quality Surveillance Program 7-1

Personnel 7-1
Specifications 7-1
Testing Kits and Methods.................................... 7-3
Tactical Petroleum Laboratory, Medium 7-3
Aviation Fuel Contamination Test Kit....................... 7-3
B2 Test Kit 7-3
Flashpoint Test Kit 7-3
Combined Contaminated Fuel Detector Kit.................. 7-3
Correlation Testing....................................... 7-3
Daily/Weekly Testing..................................... 7-3
Deterioration Limits 7-4
Testing Properties.. 7-4
Knock Values 7-4
Cetane Number.. 7-4
Color... 7-4
Corrosion 7-4
Existent Gum 7-4
Potential Gum... 7-5
Flashpoint.. 7-5
Cloud and Pour Points 7-5
Distillation 7-5
Viscosity.. 7-5
Reid Vapor Pressure 7-6
Carbon Residue.. 7-6
Bottom Sediment and Water............................... 7-6
Ash 7-7
Foam Stability... 7-7
Gravity 7-7

Water Reaction 7-7
Fuel System Icing Inhibitor Test. 7-7
Water Separometer Index Modified 7-7
Particulate Contaminant 7-7
Undissolved Water 7-8
Reclamation 7-8

Part II. Bulk Water Operations 8-1

Chapter 8. Fundamentals 8-1

Improvements to Water Support. 8-1
Concept of Bulk Water Operations. 8-1
Bulk Water Support Responsibility 8-1
Deployments. 8-1
Production and Storage. 8-1
Distribution. 8-2

Chapter 9. Water Equipment 9-1

Water Equipment End Items. 9-1
Shower Unit 9-1
Field Laundry Unit 9-1
Reverse Osmosis Water Purification Unit 9-1
Tactical Water Purification System 9-1
Medium Freshwater Purification Unit 9-2
Water Quality Analysis Set-Purification. 9-2
M149 Water Trailer 9-2
SIXCON Water Pump Module. 9-2
SIXCON Water Storage Module 9-2
Family of Water Supply Support Equipment 9-2
500-Gallon Collapsible Potable Water Drum. 9-3
3,000-Gallon Collapsible Fabric Water Tank. 9-3
20,000-Gallon Collapsible Water Tank 9-3
50,000-Gallon Collapsible Water Tank 9-3
Forward Area Water Point Supply System. 9-3
Hypochlorination Unit, Purification 9-3
350-GPM Water Pump 9-3
125-GPM Pump Set 9-4
Tank Farm Interconnection Set, Dual Tank 9-4
Tank Farm Interconnection Set, Bag Filler. 9-4
Tank Farm Interconnection Set, 4-inch Hose 9-4
Tank Farm Interconnection Set, 2-inch Hose 9-4
Tank Farm Interconnection Set, 4-inch Discharge Hose 9-4
Tank Farm Interconnection Set, Hose Nozzle 9-4
Tank Farm Interconnection Set, Accessory Kit 9-4
Tank Farm Interconnection Set, 350-GPM Pump 9-4

Tank Farm Interconnection Set, 125-GPM Pump 9-4
Tactical Water Distribution System, Pump Station 9-5
Tactical Water Distribution System, Storage Assembly 9-5
Tactical Water Distribution System, Distribution Point Assembly . . . 9-5
Tactical Water Distribution System, 600-GPM Pumping Assembly . . 9-5
Tactical Water Distribution System, 5-Mile Segment Assembly 9-5

Chapter 10. Water Support Planning **10-1**

Planning Guidance 10-1
Water Requirements 10-1
Consumption Requirements 10-1
Region 10-2
Requirements Determination 10-2

Chapter 11. Water Support Operations **11-1**

MAGTF Water Support Phases 11-1
Water Purification 11-1
Water Storage 11-1
Water Distribution 11-1
MAGTF Water Support Responsibilities 11-1
MAGTF Command Element 11-2
Other MAGTF Elements 11-2
Host Nation Considerations 11-2
Water 11-2
Refugees 11-2
Enemy Prisoners of War 11-2
Labor Force Personnel 11-3
Regional Considerations 11-3
Arid Environment 11-3
Nonarid Environment 11-3

Appendices

A   Petroleum, Oils, and Lubricants Appendix
        to the Logistics Annex A-1
B   Petroleum Allocation Defense Message System B-1
C   Bulk Petroleum Contingency Report Message
        Text Format Report C-1
D   Glossary D-1
E   References E-1

Tables

2-1. MARFOR and MAGTF Responsibilities 2-4
3-1. I/II MEF Bulk Fuel Equipment 3-7
3-2. Aircraft Fuel Delivery Capability 3-8
4-1. MAGTF Notional Fuel Requirements (Gallons) 4-3

5-1. MAGTF Storage Capability (Gallons) 5-6
7-1. Aviation Fuel Specifications 7-2
7-2. Ground Fuel Specifications 7-2
10-1. Water Requirements for Temperate Zones 10-3
10-2. Water Requirements for Tropical Zones 10-3
10-3. Water Requirements for Arctic Zones 10-4
10-4. Water Requirements for Arid Zones 10-4

Figures

3-1. Amphibious Assault Fuel System 3-2
3-2. Tactical Airfield Fuel Dispensing System 3-4
3-3. Helicopter Expedient Refueling System 3-5
4-1. MAGTF Notional Fuel Requirements (Gallons) 4-3
5-1. MAGTF Storage Capability (Gallons) 5-6

PART I. BULK FUEL OPERATIONS

CHAPTER 1. FUNDAMENTALS

Bulk fuel support is a joint venture. While bulk fuel management for joint operations is the ultimate responsibility of the joint force commander (JFC), each Service is responsible for support of its forces and any other missions assigned by the JFC. The actual procedures used to provide bulk petroleum support to the Services will depend on conditions in the area of operations (AO); for example, a developed theater or an undeveloped theater. Bulk fuel operations should adhere to applicable environmental protection rules and regulations as contained in Marine Corps Order P5090.2A, *Environmental Compliance and Protection Manual*. In the absence of local regulations, guidance contained in Department of Defense (DOD) Publication 4715.5G, *Overseas Environmental Baseline Guidance Document*, should be referenced.

Developed Theater

A mature or developed theater will usually have host nation (HN) infrastructure assets available such as pipelines, storage facilities, and railways that will help support the bulk petroleum distribution system. Airbases, tactical airfields, and Service bed-down sites will be supported by host-nation support (HNS) whenever tactically feasible. HNS will extend as far forward as possible.

Undeveloped Theater

In the undeveloped theater, HN or commercial bulk fuel facilities normally will not be available; therefore, tactical assets will have to be used. The bulk fuel supply system in the undeveloped theater may include limited tanker mooring systems, floating or submerged hose lines, and tactical fuel systems.

Resupply

Bulk fuel resupply is managed in the unified commander joint petroleum office (JPO) or subunified commander subarea petroleum office (SAPO). The combatant commander JPO coordinates all agreements concerning bulk fuel support between component commands and HNs. For the majority of places that Marine Corps forces (MARFOR) will be employed, Marines will have to make maximum use of their organic bulk fuel equipment. However, when available, HNS will be used to receive, store, and provide bulk fuel stocks to the maximum extent possible. HN assets will be used to augment United States (US) transportation and bulk fuel distribution capabilities. Once resupply lines of communications (LOCs) are established, the JPO will make preparations for resupply from continental United States (CONUS) pushed stocks and/or from theater source stocks (those contracted from theater refineries), as coordinated by either the joint task force (JTF) or the functional component commander.

Marine Corps Forces

MARFOR can obtain initial petroleum supply support from operating stocks carried aboard maritime prepositioning ships (MPSs), assault echelon and assault follow-on echelon shipping (including landing force operational reserve material), and in-theater petroleum war reserve stocks (PWRS) stored in selected storage depots throughout the theater. Additionally, maximum use will be made of available HN support bulk fuel supply systems and stocks as negotiated in standing HNS agreements. Due to the lack of tanker offloading facilities in many areas, US

Navy ship to shore (STS) capabilities may have to be utilized. Employment of the US Navy offshore petroleum discharge system (OPDS) and amphibious assault bulk fuel system (AABFS) in conjunction with the United States Marine Corps (USMC) amphibious assault fuel system (AAFS) may be required to meet Marine Corps needs. The Marine component commander or Marine expeditionary force (MEF) and the functional component commander coordinate the arrangements for this employment.

Inland Distribution

Depending upon the situation, inland distribution of bulk fuel will be by pipeline as much as possible, to include the US Army's inland petroleum distribution system (IPDS) pipeline, and by line haul as required. Whenever possible, petroleum distribution to the airfields will be by tactical hose line from the AAFS to the tactical airfield fuel dispensing system (TAFDS). Mobile refuelers will be used if required to transport bulk fuel to the airfields.

Bulk fuel support will be provided on a "push" or "pull" basis, as required, to ensure the capability of continuous operations. The basic operating concept is to keep storage tanks full at all times. For Marine Corps retail bulk fuel operations, bulk fuel will be pumped/transported from the main AAFS tank farm to the combat service support detachment (CSSD) tank farms.

CHAPTER 2. ORGANIZATION

On 1 July 1973, the Defense Logistics Agency assumed centralized management of bulk petroleum within the DOD. The Defense Energy Support Center (DESC), a component of the Defense Logistics Agency, was designated the executive agent of DOD bulk petroleum on 11 August 2004 in accordance with DOD Directive (DODD) 5101.8, *DOD Executive Agent EA (DOD EA) for Bulk Petroleum*. The combatant commanders have established JPOs to discharge staff petroleum logistic responsibilities within the theaters. Each military Service is tasked with maintaining a petroleum office to manage bulk petroleum within the Services. This chapter discusses the operational organizations and capabilities of petroleum agencies throughout the DOD.

Organization and Responsibilities

Defense Energy Support Center

The DESC is responsible for procurement of bulk petroleum products and all DOD-related energy services, and maintains the product until it is delivered to the supported Service. To provide timely and efficient support to the Services, the DESC has established regions of responsibility. These regions are located in CONUS, US Pacific Command, US European Command, and the Middle East. These regions provide close contact and coordination with the Services. In CONUS, DESC personnel order products from contractors, distribute products to the Services, and perform contract administration. Overseas, DESC personnel provide product ordering and contract administration. The missions and general functions of the DESC regions are outlined in detail in DOD Publication 4140.25-M, *DOD Management of Bulk Petroleum Products, Natural Gas, and Coal, Volumes I-IV*; and DODD 4140.25, *DOD Management Policy for Energy Commodities and Related Services*.

Unified Commands

In unified commands, staff planning and management for bulk petroleum is performed in the J-4 JPO. The JPOs are normally staffed by personnel from each department level military Service having a mission in the theater. The JPO coordinates the theater bulk petroleum operations and provides the interface between DESC and Service theater bulk petroleum managers. Service theater bulk petroleum managers provide Service bulk petroleum requirements to the JPO. The JPO consolidates the requirements for all the Services and schedules deliveries for the theater. The JPO advises the theater commander and staff on bulk petroleum logistic planning and policy matters. When required, the JPO advises the combatant commander on the allocation of bulk petroleum products and facilities.

Bulk petroleum management for the entire theater is the ultimate responsibility of the commander of the unified command through the JPO. The unified command may also establish SAPOs at the subunified command level to provide in-country or regional staff management functions.

Joint Bulk Fuel Support

During joint operations, bulk fuel management for the entire force is the ultimate responsibility of the JFC. Daily management is accomplished by the JPO or JTF petroleum staff office, in coordination with the inland distribution manager, Service retail managers, DESC, and applicable HN activities. The JFC makes the final decision on appropriate ways to accomplish bulk fuel storage and distribution to include the mix of Service tactical equipment, DESC contract support, and HNS. Services are responsible for providing retail bulk fuel support to its forces. Retail bulk fuel is fuel that is held primarily for direct support (DS) to an end-use customer such as aircraft, vehicles, etc.

Joint Task Force

Bulk petroleum management in operations is similar to that in unified commands. The JTF commander normally establishes a petroleum office within the J-4. This office coordinates the JTF bulk petroleum requirements with the unified commander JPO and the JTF components. Additional functions performed by the JTF petroleum office are to—

- Coordinate petroleum planning and operations within the JTF.
- Coordinate with the JPO for bulk petroleum requirements that must be obtained from in-country commercial sources.
- If required, establish a bulk petroleum allocation system within the JTF.

Normally, the JTF petroleum office will rely on the area unified command JPO for wholesale bulk petroleum management and support. Personnel for the JTF petroleum office are normally provided by the Services within the JTF.

Military Services

Each Service is responsible for providing retail bulk petroleum support to its forces. In addition, the Army is charged with the mission of providing overland petroleum support to all US land-based forces overseas except Navy ocean terminals. This mission includes providing the necessary force structure to construct, operate, and maintain overland pipelines in support of the wholesale theater bulk fuel mission.

The Navy, in combination with DESC, is responsible for the management of Navy ocean terminals and for STS petroleum support. In areas without an Army presence, either the dominant user designated by the joint commander, DESC (by contract), or a combination of both will be tasked to operate a bulk fuel distribution system.

US Army

The US Army staff management for petroleum planning and operations is in the US Army Petroleum Center (USAPC), Office of the Deputy Chief of Logistics. Daily operational supply of bulk fuel in the Army is managed by the USAPC. Principal duties of the USAPC include determining and consolidating Army fuel requirements, submitting procurement requests to DESC, and maintaining liaison with DESC and other military Services on operational and policy matters affecting bulk fuel operations. At the Army theater level, the theater army material management command is the item manager for bulk fuel. In accordance with DOD Publication 4140.25-M, the Army provides overland bulk fuel support to US land-based forces of all Services. The principal organization carrying out the bulk fuels distribution mission in the communications zone (COMMZ) is the petroleum group assigned directly to theater Army. The petroleum group is responsible for the detailed petroleum distribution planning that is the basis for design, construction, and operation of the distribution system for the theater. The group is responsible for liaison with HN staffs to include coordination of allied pipeline and distribution systems. The petroleum group and its subordinate units operate the bulk fuel distribution system extending from ports of entry through the COMMZ and as far into the combat zone as possible.

US Air Force

Staff management responsibility for US Air Force bulk fuel is in the Fuels Policy Branch, Deputy Chief of Staff Logistics and Engineering. Air Force Fuels Division Detachment-29 is the control point for bulk fuel requirements and inventory management. It conducts liaison with DESC and the other Services on operational and policy matters affecting bulk fuel operations. At the Air Force major command level, the Command Fuels/Supply Officer provides staff and command supervision over bulk fuel operations. In-flight refueling operations are not considered bulk fuel operations and are the responsibility of the Air Mobility Command (AMC). Organizations requiring in-flight refueling support should coordinate directly with AMC.

US Navy

Department of the Navy staff management for bulk fuel is in the Navy Energy Office, Deputy Chief of Naval Operations, Logistics. The Naval Operational Logistics Support Center (NOLSC) is the control point for bulk fuel requirements and inventory management. NOLSC duties include maintaining liaison with DESC and the other Services on operational and policy matters affecting bulk fuel operations. At the Navy major command level, fleet petroleum staff officers provide staff management on bulk fuel matters. In joint operations, the Navy supports the STS bulk fuel mission. The Navy is responsible for getting bulk fuel to the beach high water mark where the fuel is received by Army or Marine Corps bulk fuel units. The Navy's shore fuel expeditionary mission is filled entirely by ten Naval Reserve fuel units, which are equally distributed on both coasts. The units are managed by NOLSC and the expeditionary support force. Each 22-man unit is capable of handling multiple missions including bulk and retail bag farm operations, truck, aviation refueling, OPDS, and augmentation of fixed fuel facilities.

US Marine Corps

Headquarters, Marine Corps policy responsibility for bulk fuel resides in the Logistics Plans, Policies, and Strategic Mobility Division, Deputy Commandant for Installations and Logistics. NOLSC is also the Marine Corps service control point for bulk fuel. At the major command level, the Marine component commander and/or MEF assistant chief of staff G-4, is responsible for bulk fuel management, planning, operations, and policy. The Marine component commander/MEF G-4

maintains liaison with the unified command JPO, NOLSC, and other military Services on matters concerning bulk fuel operations and policy. See table 2-1 (on page 2-4) for MARFOR and Marine air-ground task force (MAGTF) responsibilities.

Marine Corps Component Commander/MEF

The Marine Corps component commander is responsible for wholesale logistic support at the Service, theater, combatant commander, and HN level. The MEF is responsible for operational and tactical bulk fuel receipt, storage, and distribution. Accordingly, the MEF will work all retail logistics provisioning for the major subordinate commands. To this end, the MEF command element (CE) is responsible for requirements determination and operations in and forward of the rear combat zone; the Marine component commander is responsible for the COMMZ and supported/supporting combatant commander coordination. All fuel operations in the MEF zone of action or amphibious objective area (AOA) will be coordinated by the MEF bulk petroleum officer. Linkage to the in-theater combatant commander JPO, DESC, HN, and other Service components is a Marine component commander responsibility.

Marine Aircraft Wing

The Marine aircraft wing (MAW) G-4 is responsible for bulk fuel planning and coordination. Within the MAW, fuel support is provided through the Marine wing support group (MWSG). The MWSG is comprised of both fixed-wing (FW) and rotary-wing (RW) Marine wing support squadrons (MWSSs). Bulk fuel operations in support of the MAW are performed by the fuel branch within the MWSS. These units provide refueling support for MAW aircraft and ground equipment. The MWSS fuel branch is responsible for the receipt, storage, distribution, and quality surveillance of bulk fuel in support of MAW operations. The fuel branch of an MWSS is capable of providing refueling support at two separate airfields simultaneously. The difference between the RW and

Table 2-1. MARFOR and MAGTF Responsibilities.

Responsibilities	MARFOR	MEF	DIV	MAW	FSSG
Plan and estimate petroleum requirements in operational plans.	X	X	X	X	X
Coordinate bulk fuel operations to ensure economy of operations and prevent duplication of functions.		X			X
Monitor fuel stocks.	X	X	X	X	X
Coordinate requirements for HNS with the combatant commander/JTF.	X	X			
Coordinate bulk fuel support for forces attached to the MEF.		X			
Request release of PWRS from Joint Chiefs of Staff via combatant commander.	X	X			
Allocate bulk fuel assets and stocks within the MEF.		X			
Identify bulk fuel shortfalls to the JTF or MARFOR.	X	X			
Plan for and establish TAFDS and helicopter expedient refueling system (HERS) support at airfields.				X	
Establish internal fuel distribution procedures.		X	X	X	X
Establish quality control procedures for bulk fuel per DOD Military Standard (MIL-STD) 3004A, *Quality Surveillance for Fuels, Lubricants, and Related Products,* and Naval Air Systems Command (NAVAIR) Publication 00-80T-109, *Aircraft Refueling Naval Air Training and Operating Procedures Standardization (NATOPS) Manual.*				X	X
Establish accounting procedures to record usage data.	X	X	X	X	X
Plan for and establish AAFS sites as required to support the MEF.	X	X			X
Coordinate STS bulk fuel operations.	X	X			X
Plan for and establish distribution of bulk fuel to support the MEF.	X	X		X	X
Coordinate bulk fuel requirements with the MEF-G-4. Ensure stocks are sufficient to reach and maintain stockage objectives.			X	X	X
Provide bulk fuel laboratory support to the MEF.					X
Coordinate bulk fuel supply for HN/other established.	X	X		X	X

FW fuel branches is the table of equipment. (For current quantities, refer to the Logistic Management Information System.)

Marine Division

The Marine division (MARDIV) is a fuel user, not a fuel provider. However, the MARDIV has limited organic bulk fuel assets to support its own units.

Force Service Support Group

The force service support group (FSSG) provides bulk fuel supply support for the sustainment of the MEF. It provides all bulk fuel support that is beyond the organic capabilities of supported units. Bulk fuel planning and coordination is performed in the FSSG G-3. To conduct bulk fuel operations, the FSSG uses bulk fuel assets located within the engineer and motor transport organizations.

Engineer Support Battalion. The engineer support battalion (ESB) is responsible for providing general bulk fuel support to the MEF to include receipt, storage, distribution, and quality surveillance. The ESB has one bulk fuel company to provide this support. When supporting MAGTF airfields, the ESB is responsible for fuel distribution to the airfield. The bulk fuel company of the ESB provides coordination and control with the MAW for transfer of bulk fuel to the airfields.

Transportation Support Battalion. The general support (GS) company and DS company in the transportation support battalion provide the transportation and distribution of bulk fuel for the MEF.

CHAPTER 3. TACTICAL FUEL SYSTEMS

Marine Corps bulk fuel equipment has to meet a wide spectrum of requirements from STS operations to aircraft refueling. To meet these requirements, the Marine Corps has developed a family of tactical fuel systems (TFSs). Each system is designed and configured specifically to support a unique mission requirement using similar components. The ability to alter fundamental system configurations and interchangeability of components allows the creation of limitless combinations of tailored systems to meet mission requirements.

The Marine Corps family of TFSs was originally designed and deployed in the 1950s to replace the 55-gallon drum and 5-gallon fuel can as the primary method for MARFOR's bulk fuel support. The basic design of collapsible fuel tanks, trailer-mounted pumps, fuel hoses and valves, filtration vessels, and miscellaneous components has provided a solid foundation for the evolution of the family of TFSs to meet the ever changing operational and tactical fuel support requirements of the MAGTF. Today the family of TFSs provides a wide range of storage tank sizes ranging from 500-gallon to 50,000-gallon capacities with receipt and pumping rates ranging from 125 gallons per minute (GPM) to 600 GPM.

Amphibious Assault Fuel System

The AAFS (USMC table of authorized materiel control number [TAMCN] B0685) is the largest TFS. Consisting of many assemblies, the AAFS is used to receive, store, transfer, and dispense all types of fuel. The AAFS supplies bulk fuel to all elements of a MAGTF including distribution by hose line to airfields. The system can receive fuel from offshore vessels, railcars, tank trucks, bulk storage tanks, pipeline/hose line, and drums. Fuel is stored and can be transferred to another storage site or dispensed to individual containers, vehicles, tank trucks, and other fuel systems. Six assemblies compose the AAFS:

- Beach unloading.
- Receiving.
- Two booster stations.
- Two adapting.
- Two dispensing.
- Six tank farms.

Each AAFS has one beach unloading assembly used for receiving fuel during STS operations. Two booster station assemblies in each AAFS are used when the distance between storage sites is greater than the pumping distance. The AAFS storage capacity comes from the six tank farms. One receiving assembly in each AAFS provides the capability to receive fuel from multiple sources. Two dispensing assemblies in each AAFS provide the capability to dispense fuel. The AAFS has two adapting assemblies to make the system compatible with commercial and other Services' fuel systems. Versatility is an important part of the AAFS, which can be deployed as a whole or tailored to meet mission requirements.

The AAFS storage capacity is 1.12 million gallons made up from its six tank farms. The AAFS has approximately 5 miles of 6-inch assault hose and uses 600-GPM pumping capabilities. Using quick-connect, cam-lock fittings, the AAFS can be assembled without tools and is compatible with the other Marine Corps TFSs. See figure 3-1 on page 3-2.

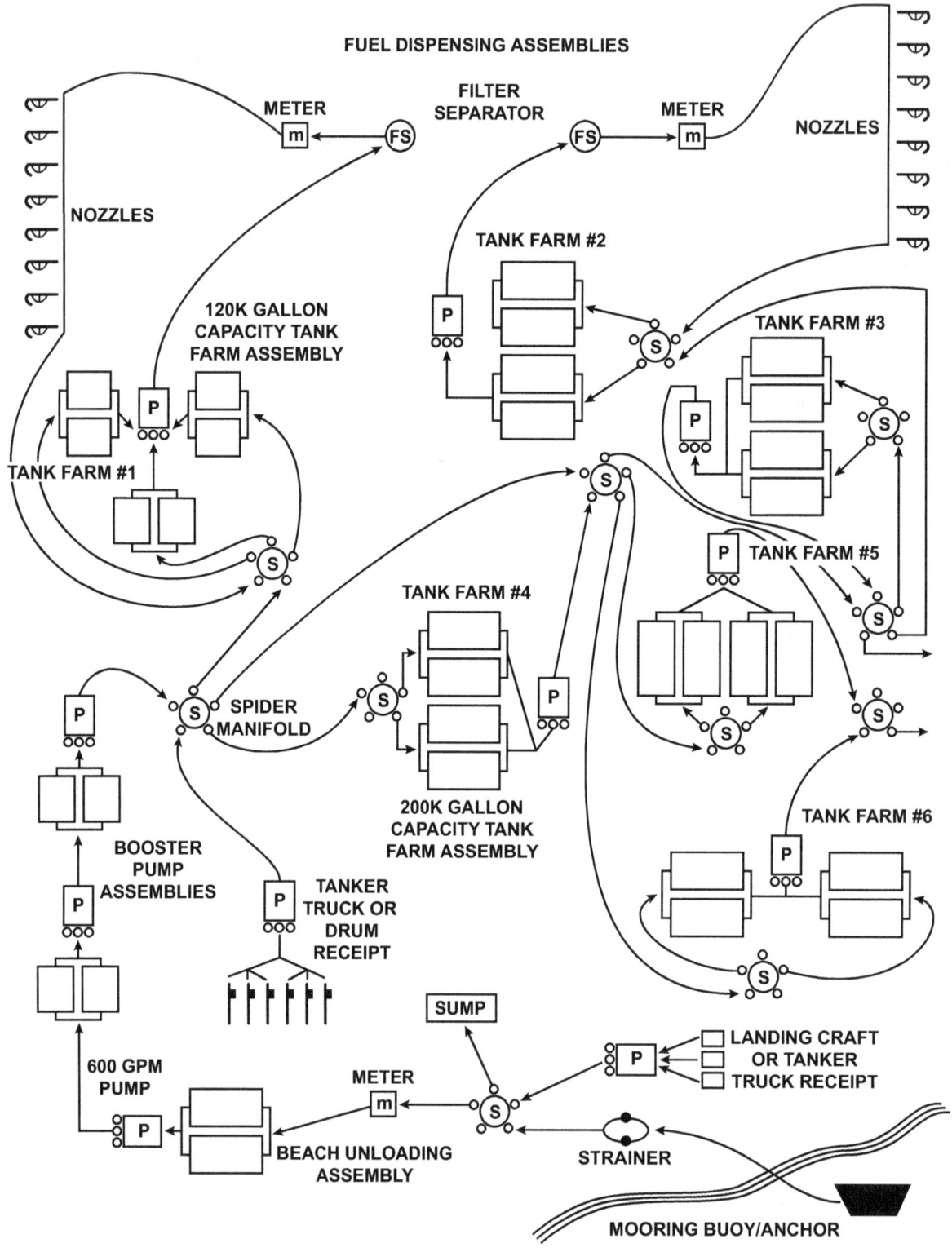

Figure 3-1. Amphibious Assault Fuel System.

Tactical Airfield Fuel Dispensing System

The tactical airfield fuel dispensing system (TAFDS) (USMC TAMCN B0675) is similar in design to the AAFS. This system is used for receiving, storing, transferring, and dispensing aviation fuel in support of expeditionary airfields. This system is air transportable, versatile, and can be quickly assembled. Compatible with other Marine Corps TFSs, the TAFDS can receive fuel from almost any source with the appropriate adapters. Fifty-five gallon drums may be defueled using the drum-unloading portion of the TAFDS. With the single fuel on the battlefield concept, the TAFDS can supply aviation and ground fuel for airfields.

The TAFDS consists of six 20,000-gallon and four 50,000-gallon collapsible tanks for a storage capacity of 320,000 gallons. Each TAFDS rates seven pumps of either 350 or 600 GPM. With its designed pumping rate and equipment to set up 12 dispensing points, the TAFDS has a multiplane fueling capability. The TAFDS may also be used to replenish tank vehicles. Filtration of the fuel to meet naval air requirements is accomplished using filter separators and fuel quality monitors. The TAFDS is used for hot or cold aircraft refueling. See figure 3-2 on page 3-4.

Helicopter Expedient Refueling System

The helicopter expedient refueling system (HERS) (USMC TAMCN B1135) is designed for support of helicopter operations in advanced areas and remote sites. It is normally used at forward arming and refueling points (FARPs). Key elements of the HERS are versatility, transportability, and rapid setup. Equipped with 2-inch hoses and adapters, the HERS is compatible with other Marine Corps TFSs. The HERS has a maximum capacity of 18,000 gallons, utilizing 18 500-gallon collapsible drums and 3 3,000-gallon collapsible tanks. The HERS has four 100/125 GPM pumps and enough components to set up four refueling points. It may be deployed as a whole or in part to meet operational requirements. Due to the limited storage capacity and the flow rate of the HERS (100 GPM), it is best used for attack helicopters to increase their range, but can also be used to support utility helicopters. See figure 3-3 on page 3-5.

Expedient Refueling System

The expedient refueling system (ERS) (USMC TAMCN B1570) was designed for support of ground vehicles in advanced positions. The ERS is easily transportable and highly mobile. It is normally used with 500-gallon collapsible fuel drums or 3,000-gallon collapsible fuel tanks. It consists of either a 100 or 125 GPM pump with various 2-inch hoses and fittings for two refueling points. All components within the ERS have 2-inch couplings. The ERS does not have filtration equipment and should not be used for aircraft refueling.

Six Containers Together

The Marine Corps liquid storage, transporting, and dispensing system is commonly called a SIXCON [six containers together]. Certain SIXCONs are used to store, transport, and dispense fuel. A SIXCON is transportable by air or ground. Components of the fuel SIXCON system are a fuel pump module and five fuel tank modules. The modules form a fuel distribution source that can be transported as a unit or individually.

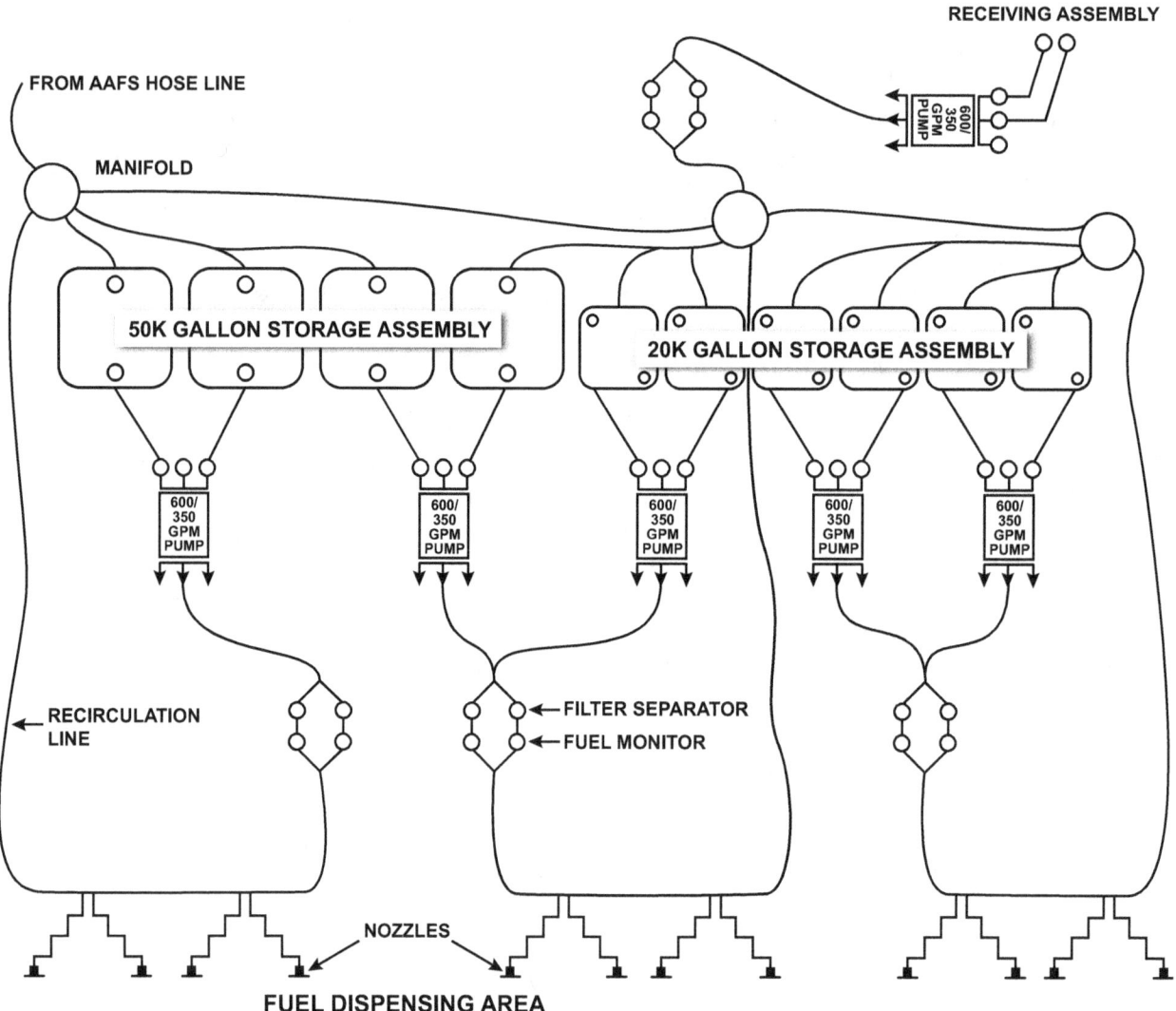

Figure 3-2. Tactical Airfield Fuel Dispensing System.

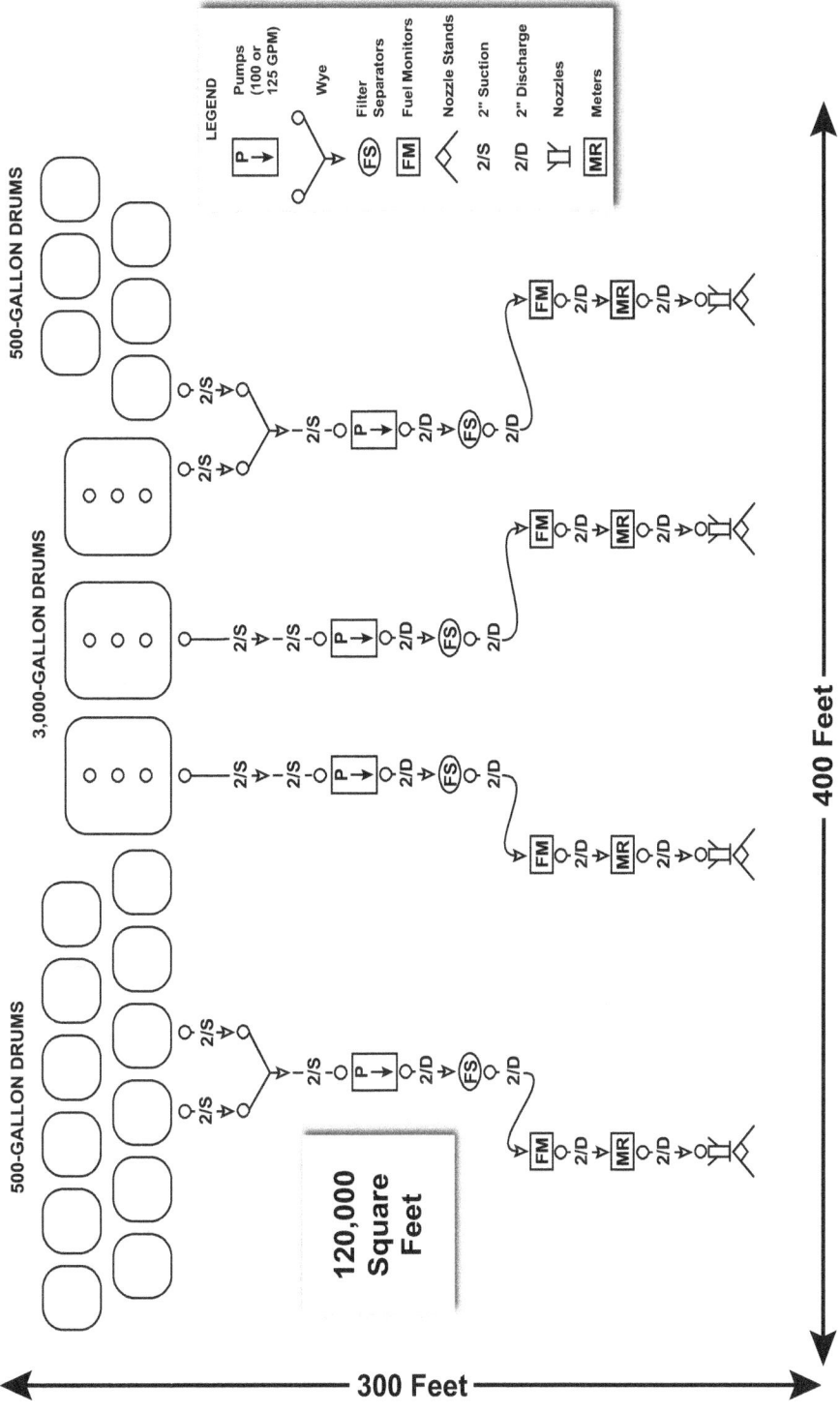

Figure 3-3. Helicopter Expedient Refueling System.

Fuel Pump Module

The SIXCON fuel pump module (USMC TAMCN B1580) consists of a 125-GPM pump, 100-GPM filter separator, 100-GPM fuel quality monitor, meter assembly, and hose reel. The fuel pump was designed to dispense fuel from several types of fuel tanks, for either defueling or for filtering aircraft or ground fuels. The rate of transfer for the SIXCON pump module is up to 100 GPM.

Fuel Tank Modules

Each SIXCON fuel tank module (USMC TAMCN B2085) is made of stainless steel and has a capacity of 900 gallons. It is encased by a steel frame that allows stacking and connecting to form an 8- by 8- by 20-foot International Organization for Standardization (ISO) container. The fuel tank is equipped with all the hoses and adapters to connect the tanks to the pump unit.

Accessories

SIXCON modules are interconnected using special horizontal and vertical ISO connectors. Fuel is transferred via 2-inch hoses with dry-break couplings. This allows rapid assembly and disassembly without loss of fuel or damage to the environment.

Cyclic Resupply

SIXCON modules are assigned to all elements of the MAGTF. These organizations may implement a cyclic resupply procedure where full modules are exchanged for empty ones. SIXCONs may also be assigned to using organizations for minimal fuel handling at the operator level.

M970 Mobile Refueler

The M970 5,000-gallon mobile refueler (USMC TAMCN D0215) provides aircraft refueling/defueling and over-the-road transportation of bulk fuel. It is assigned to both the aviation combat element (ACE) and the combat service support element (CSSE). Within the ACE, the M970 is organic to the MWSS and is used primarily to refuel aircraft. Within the CSSE, the M970 is organic to the transportation support battalion and is assigned to CSSE motor transport and/or engineer detachments. The CSSE uses the M970 to transport bulk fuel between storage sites or directly to the customer.

Tactical Petroleum Laboratory, Medium

The tactical petroleum laboratory, medium (TPLM) (USMC TAMCN B0695) provides the essential testing components integrated into an ISO container to monitor the critical physical and chemical characteristics of aviation and ground fuels. There are 16 tests that can be conducted in accordance with the American Society for Testing and Materials (ASTM). JP-4, JP-5, JP-8, diesel, and their commercial grade equivalents can be tested for composition and quality against minimum standards as specified in DOD MIL-STD 3004A. The TPLM can also test captured fuels.

USMC Aircraft Bulk Fuel Handling Systems

Air-to-air refueling or transfer of bulk aviation fuel can both extend the range of aircraft and provide a means for the MAGTF to "air deliver" jet fuel to forward operating sites. *(NOTE: Jet fuel can also be used as diesel fuel.)* Table 3-1 is a listing of I/II MEF bulk fuel equipment.

USMC KC-130R Transport

The primary mission of the KC-130R Transport is air-to-air refueling. It can air-to-air refuel tactical Marine FW aircraft, CH-53 helicopters, and MV-22s. The KC-130R can also land at distant airfields carrying up to 10,000 gallons of jet fuel.

Table 3-1. I/II MEF Bulk Fuel Equipment.

Unit	AAFS	TAFDS	HERS	500-Gal Drums	Pump SIXCON	Tank SIXCON	M970	TPLM
FSSG	8	0	0	56	~52	188	20	4
MWSS FW (2)	0	12	4	In HERS	4	18	20	0
MWSS RW (2)	0	8	14	In HERS	2	12	20	0
TOTAL	8	20	18	56	~58	218	60	2
~ = approximately								

Tactical Bulk Fuel Distribution System

The tactical bulk fuel distribution system (TBFDS) consists of full range extension tanks, hoses, and couplings that can be loaded internally on a CH-53 helicopter. This system can be used to extend the operating range of the CH-53 or allow for helicopter delivery of fuel to distant forward areas. The TBFDS-configured CH-53 can refuel aircraft at FARPs or refuel diesel engine ground vehicles and equipment. This system is installed and operated by aircrew personnel. It contains three 800-gallon tanks, for a maximum storage capacity of 2,400 gallons.

Aviation Refueling Capability

The aviation refueling capability (ARC) (USMC TAMCN D0210) is a 5,000-gallon commercial refueler modified for Marine Corps use. The ARC provides a mobile aviation refueling capability to the MAW. The ARC has been procured through a General Services Administration contract. The fielding of the ARC and a subsequent off-road aviation refueling system enable the Marine Corps to phase the aged M970 semi-trailer out of the inventory. The M970 was fielded in the 1970s, with a follow on buy in 1994, and is experiencing readiness problems. The ARC provides the M970 basic capabilities with several technological advancements, however, the ARC has limited off-road capabilities. Therefore each MAW must still maintain three M970s per MWSS.

Joint Service Interoperability

Joint support to the MAGTF may include providing or receiving fuel support from other Services, foreign forces, or commercial sources. The MAGTF CE is responsible for coordinating bulk fuel support for the MAGTF. Joint bulk fuel interoperability is addressed in Joint Publication (JP) 4-03, *Joint Bulk Petroleum and Water Doctrine*.

US Navy Ship to Shore Systems

Initial phases of amphibious or maritime prepositioning force operations may require bulk fuel delivery from STS. Both amphibious ships and MPSs squadrons (MPSRONs) employ floating hose lines to provide bulk fuel issue via STS operations. Additionally, the OPDS can be employed to support and sustain MAGTF or JTF operations ashore.

Amphibious Assault Bulk Fuel System

The AABFS provides a fuel line from the supplying ship to the high water mark ashore where the fuel lines are connected to shore-based bulk fuel systems of the landing force. The AABFS consists of buoyant, 6-inch (diameter) reinforced rubber hose lines up to 10,000 feet in length. Two or more buoyant lines can be connected to achieve greater distances between the ship and the shoreline. However, they require floating booster stations to perform fuel transfer when the distance is more than 5,000 feet. Buoyant hose systems are employed to support the initial phases of amphibious landings. An AABFS can be installed in 4 to 6 hours under favorable surf conditions.

Offshore Petroleum Discharge System

The OPDS is designed to discharge petroleum products to USMC AAFS, US Army tactical petroleum terminals, or US Army IPDS pipelines. The OPDS can be installed up to 4 statute miles offshore and support STS fuel replenishment rates of up to 1.2 million gallons per day (based on a 20-hour operating day). If the ship standoff distance is less than 2 statute miles, dual lines can be used resulting in faster product transfer.

The OPDS can produce delivery rates of 1,000 GPM. The OPDS includes the initial fuel tanker (ship) that provides the initial delivery of fuel (up to 15 million gallons) and the mooring apparatus for itself and follow-on tankers. The OPDS employs either a four-point moor or a single anchor leg mooring with surface buoy to allow the ship to moor and "weather vane" in the prevailing winds in a 360-degree arc.

Military Sealift Command civilian crews install the system with the assistance of naval support personnel. Besides underwater divers and support personnel from an amphibious construction battalion, the system requires side-loadable warping tugs and/or powered or non-powered causeway sections to conduct the installation.

US Army Petroleum System

Theater support may be provided from US Army fuel sources. Fuel support, which includes interface with Marine Corps TFSs, must be planned and coordinated in advance. The selection of specific systems depends on the projected requirements. The US Army theater fuel manager coordinates fuel delivery requirements. When operating with the US Air Force, the US Army can airdrop fuel in quantities up to 10,000 gallons in support of operating forces. Fuel support equipment employed may include US Army tactical petroleum terminals, IPDS or line haul vehicles.

US Air Force Air-based Petroleum System

Refueler aircraft and aircraft equipped with aerial bulk fuel delivery systems may be required to support MAGTF operations. Support capability ranges from air delivery of packaged fuel (500-gallon collapsible drums) to bulk fuel pumped from transport aircraft or aircraft internal tanks. See table 3-2. Wet-wing refueling/defueling methods may be prescribed for special mission support operations. These methods may range from the transfer of jet fuel from a delivery aircraft to receiving tactical storage systems or into a receiving aircraft.

Table 3-2. Aircraft Fuel Delivery Capability.

Type Aircraft	500-Gal Drum Delivery Model and Gallon Capacity	Wet-Wing Delivery Model and Gallon Capacity
C-130	5,000	4,400
C-141	9,000	12,500
C-5A/B	27,000	29,000

CHAPTER 4. BULK FUEL PLANNING

Normally, bulk fuel capabilities are spread throughout the MAGTF. This is especially true of bulk fuel distribution capabilities. But with the smaller forces of today, there is often a benefit to consolidating the bulk fuel assets. For example, if a mobile refueler was controlled by a central organization, it could be used to support several units and would be used to the maximum extent possible. This would not be true if each unit had its own mobile refueler. The MAGTF has also provided central organizations within the ACE and the CSSE for its bulk liquids storage requirements.

To be effective, the overall bulk fuel effort needs to be planned and coordinated at the MAGTF level as early as possible and continue throughout the operation.

Planning Requirements

Planning for bulk fuel support can be a complex and challenging task. Time, space, distances, terrain, resources, and the operating environment are all planning factors that have to be considered. There are six major elements of bulk fuel planning: requirements, sourcing and procurement, transportation, storage, distribution, and equipment.

Requirements

Determining bulk fuel requirements is one of the most important planning elements for bulk fuel support. Requirements have to be determined before any of the other elements can be effectively considered. Requirements will be the main factor in deciding equipment, personnel, and stockage objectives.

Sourcing and Procurement

Determining the source and provider of bulk fuel stocks to the MAGTF or MARFOR varies greatly depending on the situation. Before deploying, the planner needs to coordinate fuel sources and establish resupply procedures.

Transportation

Planning for bulk fuel transportation involves movement of fuel from the fuel source to the Marine Corps bulk fuel sites. This is usually a wholesale function that will be arranged in coordination with the JPO, MAGTF fuels officer, and the theater area support command. Transportation methods include ships, railcars, tank trucks, pipeline, and aircraft.

Storage

Planning for bulk fuel storage requires a consideration of requirements, stockage objectives, and the frequency of resupply. The JFC prescribes bulk fuel supply levels for the theater in day(s) of supply (DOS). Marine component and/or MAGTF commanders prescribe supply levels for Marine forces based on requirements and equipment availability. When operating in a joint environment, the Marine Corps planners must plan for the supply levels of all organizations that it may be supporting.

Distribution

Distribution consists of transporting fuel from the bulk storage site to the using units. Distribution can also be called the retail end of the transportation system.

Equipment

The bulk fuel equipment required to support the mission is based on the other five elements for bulk fuel planning. Planning for bulk fuel equipment must include both stationary and mobile bulk fuel equipment.

Planning Considerations

The bulk fuel supply system must be designed according the mission, terrain, and climate. The planner must consider the following:

- Capability of installations and/or unit (to include HN) to provide the required support.
- Time to construct an operational bulk fuel system.
- Requirements for bulk fuel storage facilities, offshore unloading facilities, pipeline/hose line, and distribution points.
- Availability of bulk fuel units and other units needed to construct, install, operate, and maintain the bulk fuel system.
- Terrain, since this impacts both the ability to install the bulk fuel system and fuel usage factors.

Planning for Joint Bulk Fuel Operations

The supported combatant commander and/or the JFC are responsible for the overall planning of bulk fuel logistical support. The unified or joint command plan is the basis for all subordinate bulk fuel support plans. This plan establishes concepts, objectives, and missions, and allocates available resources. Operation plans submitted to the joint staff will include a Petroleum, Oils, and Lubricants Appendix to the Logistics Annex in the format prescribed in Chairman of the Joint Chiefs of Staff Manual 3122.03A, *Joint Operation Planning and Execution System (JOPES)*,

Volume II, Planning Formats and Guidance. See appendix A. Once the concept is approved by the JFC, the Service components then prepare the implementing bulk fuel support plan. During operations, the joint staff and the Service bulk fuel planners revise the basic plans as required to support the mission.

Army Petroleum Group

Normally, the Army petroleum group or designated dominant Service is responsible for theater bulk fuel planning and the theater inland petroleum distribution plan. This planning is done in concert with the component Services' bulk fuel plans. The theater inland petroleum distribution plan is prepared and published as an annex to the theater logistic support plan.

Compatibility

During joint operations, the compatibility between the Services' bulk fuel systems is a key factor. Compatibility must be addressed during the planning cycle with emphasis on the following interfaces:

- STS offload facilities.
- Land-based distribution systems and mobile refueling equipment.

Marine Corps Bulk Fuel Planning

The Marine Corps must maintain the ability to deploy rapidly to a variety of environments and tactical situations. Once in place, Marine Corps forces must be able to operate with a full spectrum of bulk fuel support. A key factor to successful bulk fuel planning is early coordination between the fuel planners and the operators. To develop an effective fuel plan, the planners must have a good understanding of the commander's concept of operations and the tactical equipment being used.

Determine Requirements

The first step is to collect fuel requirement data from each element of the MAGTF so the planner can estimate the fuel requirements for Marine forces. While this is not intended to be an exact figure, it does need to be as accurate as possible because of the large impact fuel requirements have on other planning elements.

Automated Systems

Data provided by automated systems must be validated by fuel planners using equipment densities and consumption rates.

Time Phasing

An equally important function of bulk fuel requirements identification is time phasing. Bulk fuel requirements must be time phased to coordinate transportation, storage, and distribution. Time-phased requirements begin with a determination of daily requirements in the objective area. This includes daily demand, storage capacity, throughput capability, and time delay from initial request until delivery.

Methods of Computing Fuel Requirements

All MAGTF elements are responsible for estimating their fuel requirements and submitting them to the fuel planners in a timely manner. Fuel requirements should be computed at the staff level based on historical data, equipment density, time, and operational tempo. Fuel planners need to provide specific guidance to the units on the procedures to be followed. The guidance should provide data concerning hours-per-day, gallons per hour (GPH), resupply times, DOS on hand, and operational tempo. The bulk fuel staff officers will review requirements submissions for accuracy.

Most units in the fuel community have developed automated tools such as spreadsheets to assist in the fuel planning. These tools should be available from the MEF bulk liquids sections or the Marine Corps Detachment, Fort Lee, VA.

Aviation fuel requirements are computed using aircraft characteristic manuals. This method takes into account the operational tempo, sortie rates, sortie lengths, and fuel rates for each type of aircraft. It is also recommended that aviation fuel requirements be computed at the staff level based on the aircraft density and the operational tempo provided from the G-3/S-3. The bulk fuel staff officers will review requirements submissions for accuracy.

Notional MAGTF Bulk Fuel Requirements

Notional fuel requirements are often used during planning, especially before an equipment list has been generated or compiled. Notional fuel requirements are based on established fuel consumption rates and hours per day for equipment in participating units.

Notional requirements are for initial planning only and should never be used for detailed planning or for procuring fuel stocks. Table 4-1 is the notional fuel requirements for various MAGTFs. The data is from MAGTF II, Logistics Automated Information System.

Table 4-1. MAGTF Notional Fuel Requirements (Gallons).

Force Size	Daily Fuel Requirements (Assault Rate)	Daily Fuel Requirements (Sustained Rate)
Marine Expeditionary Force (MEF)	1,204,856	950,010
Marine Expeditionary Brigade (MEB)	563,868	443,738
Marine Expeditionary Unit (MEU)	63,842	48,145

Sourcing and Procurement

Marine planners must be aware of the various agencies and procedures for procuring bulk fuel. The sources of bulk fuel procurement are as varied as the possible missions and objectives that could be assigned a MAGTF. After analyzing fuel requirements, the Marine planner turns to the theater petroleum manager or joint staff to coordinate fuel sourcing and transportation.

Transportation

Transportation planning may include commercial contracted hauling, railway tankers, shipping, other Service assets and pipeline availability. MAGTF planners should look at all available transportation assets in the area and plan for adequate tactical transportation assets to be deployed in a timely manner. These transportation assets are also key elements in determining the fuel support equipment and personnel required. If the fuel source is close and transportation is readily available, the planner may not have to provide as much storage capacity. If the LOCs are long and resupply is not timely, the planner may have to increase the stockage objective, which means storage equipment will have to be increased.

Transportation often represents the greatest challenge to the logistical field due to the high demand for transportation assets.

Storage

The fuel planner must consider storage and distribution assets required and personnel to operate and maintain them. Storage requirements are based on the anticipated usage by a supported unit and the stockage objective as established by the commander. Stock levels to be stored will depend on consumption rates, resupply methods, transportation assets, and distribution systems. Storage methods, land requirements, and security are the key factors in storage planning. It is important that the bulk fuel storage equipment be scheduled for delivery to the operating area in order to allow for installation of the storage systems in time to support the transportation schedule.

Distribution

Distribution is often the most difficult of the bulk fuel missions. Equipment, time-phased requirements, and distance are the main factors affecting distribution. Distribution problems will normally become more complex the longer the operation, the greater the consumption rates, and the farther inland the MAGTF goes. Resupply concepts of unit distribution versus supply point distribution will also affect the type and amount of resources needed to support bulk fuel distribution to the MAGTF.

War Reserve Requirements and Stocks

Petroleum War Reserve Requirement

To ensure the supply of petroleum products in the initial phases of a contingency, the unified commands and the Services develop requirements to size petroleum war reserve stocks properly. The petroleum war reserve requirement (PWRR) is based on the need to support specific contingency operations until normal LOCs are established and resupply arrangements are in place. The joint staff develops guidelines, approved by the Office of the Secretary of Defense, on DOS and appropriate assumptions on secure sources of resupply. These guidelines are provided to the Services and combatant commanders and serve as the basis for determining requirements. Using these guidelines, the Services develop and apply structured, auditable methods of computing PWRR for each approved theater/command operation plan (OPLAN).

Petroleum War Reserve Stocks

PWRS are the on-hand product designated to satisfy PWRR. This stockage is in addition to the peacetime operating stock for each location.

Commanders of unified commands are authorized to release or reallocate PWRS in emergency situations. PWRS are usually stored in theater and are monitored by the appropriate combatant commander JPO/SAPO.

MEF Petroleum War Reserve Requirement

The MEF computes PWRR based on the time period, contingency location, and type of product required. The joint staff also establishes prepositioning objectives for regions and areas worldwide in the form of combat days of petroleum supply to be maintained in accordance with DODD 4140.25. These objectives consider such factors as wartime tanker sailing times, in theater distribution times, attrition factors, and appropriate safety levels. As a result, the amount of bulk fuel PWRR (DOS) that the MEF can register varies depending on the theater in which the MEF is operating. The MEF will usually have less than 60 DOS of bulk fuel as accompanying supplies or PWRS, and resupply will begin at a date earlier than D+60.

Consolidated Defense Fuel Support Points

The DESC consolidates military Service PWRR for storage at defense fuel support points and assigns maximum and minimum storage levels in the inventory management plan (IMP). In consonance with approved stock fund operating plans and budgets, it is possible that the entire amount of PWRS that the MEF is authorized in a particular theater may not be sourced. If the MARFOR have a bulk fuel shortfall, the Marine component commander will notify the appropriate unified commander's JPO. The document that identifies the amount of PWRS allocated to the MEF is the DESC IMP. The IMP contains the MEF PWRR by location and identifies the PWRS that are sourced to meet that requirement. The Marine component G-4 and MEF bulk liquids section maintain current copies of the IMP, and it is also available via the classified SECRET Internet Protocol Router Network (SIPRNET).

Prepositioned PWRS

DESC will attempt to preposition PWRS at the terminal location nominated by the military Service. Where storage or operational conditions are limited, DESC will locate stocks, at the most appropriate alternate terminal, following coordination with the unified command and the requiring military Service. Malpositioned stocks will be counted against the total PWRR. However, these stocks may not be counted as DOS available at the point of planned use during assessment of OPLANs capability.

CHAPTER 5. BULK FUEL THEATER OPERATIONS

In theater operations, the MAGTF commander may be part of a developed or undeveloped theater. Bulk fuel support concerns and requirements are addressed according to the development stage of a theater. The three main objectives of bulk fuel support are supplying fuel when needed, distributing fuel where needed, and providing fuel resupply on time. When the MAGTF is involved in a sustained operation ashore, bulk fuel operations are deployed in three phases: development, lodgment, and build-up.

Developed Theater

In a developed theater, an existing bulk fuel distribution system is usually available to help support MARFOR. The existing system helps offset the requirements for Marine Corps TFSs. A developed theater usually consists of tanker unloading facilities, terminals, pipelines, pump stations, dispensing facilities, and rail tank car facilities.

Actual procedures for accomplishing the delivery of bulk fuel to the user will vary between theaters. Civilian personnel or the theater Army will normally operate these facilities. However, Marine Corps bulk fuel units could be tasked with operating the facilities, particularly during the early phases of operations before the theater Army has all its assigned forces.

Pipeline System

In a developed theater, the pipeline system usually extends into the Army corps rear with hose line extensions into Army corps storage sites and Marine Corps force combat service support (CSS) areas and airfields. When practical, branch lines from the pipeline are used to supply major users such as Marine Corps CSSDs and MWSSs.

Military tank trucks and commercial vehicles, if required and available, can supplement the pipeline/hose line system.

Theater Stockage Objectives

In a developed theater, most of the theater stockage objectives are usually held in fixed facility storage tanks. This reduces the quantity of bulk fuel that the Marine Corps would need to store in tactical bulk fuel systems. Theater stockage objectives will vary between theaters depending on planned operational contingency anticipated usage rates. Marine forces stockage objectives held in tactical fuel systems will depend on resupply times from theater storage and the daily fuel requirement.

Undeveloped Theater

Providing fuel support in an undeveloped theater presents many problems not faced in a developed area. TFSs have to be brought into the area and mooring facilities, storage facilities, pipeline, and/or hose lines have to be installed. During the early stages of an operation, forces have to rely on their organic equipment and personnel. As the operation progresses, additional equipment and personnel are brought in to expand the fuel system. A TFS capable of supporting the mission is developed in the area when practical. Initial fuel storage facilities should be expanded when possible so floating storage (tankers or barges) holding reserve fuel for shore units may be released.

Any available commercial or HNS will be considered for use as part of the bulk fuel system. Use of these systems and their bulk fuel products should be obtained through DESC contracts, local purchase procedures, or through HNS agreements.

Minimum Bulk Fuel Stockage Objective

The minimum bulk fuel stockage objective for the undeveloped theater is 15 DOS. This includes bulk fuel stored in tactical equipment and off-shore shipping or floating dumps. Fuel is distributed from beach storage by hose line, tank vehicles, helicopters, and any other means available. As the fuel system is developed, it will consist of hose lines and collapsible storage tanks. The primary method of receiving bulk fuel in the undeveloped theater will be STS operations using Navy shipping with the AABFS or the OPDS, tanker vehicles, barges, or any other suitable transportation asset.

Tactical Hose Line

Large users such as tactical airfields are supplied by tactical hose line when possible. The tactical hose line and/or pipeline will extend as far forward as possible, usually into the Army corps rear area, to reduce mobile transport requirements. Although hose lines are the most rapid and easily deployed system, a more permanent system is normally installed if the system must stay in place for long periods. When possible, the rear area COMMZ, corps support, and force service support areas will be established. In the early stages, the theater may only consist of a JTF support area, MEF forward area with CSSDs, or Army division support area, and later an Army corps support area. The rear area COMMZ may never be formed depending on the duration of the operation.

Air Lines of Communications

In the early stages of an undeveloped theater, there is often a requirement to support forces with air lines of communications (ALOC). The Air Force AMC provides this support with C-130, C-141, C-5A, and C-17 aircraft. Requirements for ALOC support are coordinated through channels established in the OPLANs. If the forces advance using air assets, then normally the ALOC is required to support them. The

following types of aerial bulk fuel support are available from the AMC.

Packaged Products

The 5-gallon fuel cans and 55-gallon drums may be internally loaded in cargo aircraft for delivery to airfields near the units being supported.

Airdrop

When suitable aircraft loading and unloading areas are not available, fuel may be airdropped or delivered by low-altitude parachute extraction systems. A 500-gallon collapsible drum can be transported internally or externally to deliver fuel.

Aerial Bulk Fuel Delivery System

The Air Force and Marine Corps have aircraft specially equipped with internal collapsible tanks and a pump for deliveries of bulk fuels into areas where suitable landing sites are available.

Wet Wing Refueling

The C-130, C-141, C-5A, and C-17 aircraft have internal pumps for defueling. Using Marine Corps or Army ground equipment (hoses and nozzles), these aircraft can deliver aviation fuel into Marine Corps or Army storage containers located at suitable landing areas. Refer to table 3-2, page 3-8.

Tactical Bulk Fuel Delivery System

This system is installed and operated by aircrew personnel. It contains three 800-gallon tanks, for a maximum storage capacity of 2,400 gallons. It can be used at forward sites to dispense fuel to other aircrafts or ground vehicles.

Phases of Bulk Fuel Operations

During sustained operations ashore (SOA), tactical bulk fuel equipment must be deployed to provide support to the MAGTF. To best support the

MAGTF, bulk fuel operations should be conducted in three phases: development, lodgment, and build-up.

Development

Due to the high consumption and limited bulk fuel capabilities, the development phase is often the most critical phase of bulk fuel operations. The commander and staff need to look closely at the full range of the vehicles going ashore, the time-phased resupply available, and the equipment available to support the MAGTF during this phase. The development phase may be initiated as an airborne, airmobile, amphibious assault, or an uncontested debarkation at a friendly port.

The first units of the MAGTF entering an operational area will probably carry only enough bulk fuel for immediate purposes. Resupply of these units must begin rapidly. During initial deployment, fuel will probably be provided in prepackaged containers (drums and cans), 500-gallon tanks, SIXCONs, and mobile refuelers, then delivered to the AOA by surface or air from offshore amphibious ships. These items must be continually recovered and sent back to the source to be reused. All bulk fuel resources within the AOA must be considered and exploited during this phase.

Lodgment

The lodgment phase involves the establishment and expansion of bulk fuel transportation, storage, and distribution systems. Shore basing the MAGTF, arrival of assault follow-on echelon, and sustainment operations will increase the demand beyond the capabilities of those systems deployed during the development phase. Larger bulk fuel systems will have to be established ashore to handle the requirements of the MAGTF.

Build-up

Once the lodgment phase is established, build-up of the bulk fuel systems can begin. The mission and the commander's intent as to required stockage objective on the ground would dictate the final requirement for the bulk fuel systems.

Bulk Fuel Operations Within the MAGTF

In accordance with *Strategy 21*, the future Marine Corps forces will be scalable with additional emphasis on expeditionary capabilities. The emphasis on these capabilities includes a refinement of over-the-horizon amphibious assault capabilities, increased flexibility of maritime prepositioning forces, fast and flexible schemes of maneuver for the ground combat element (GCE), and development of an ACE composed predominantly of short takeoff and vertical landing aircraft.

Expeditionary operations will require compatible concepts of bulk fuel support. One concept that may not be compatible is the "large footprint on the beach." This concept takes time to establish and it limits flexibility. If bulk fuel supply operations are to be conducted with only a minimal build-up ashore, the emphasis should be on proper planning and operational management. Employing the most compatible concept, along with accurate planning and efficient operations, should ensure that units ashore do not run out of fuel nor become saddled with excess bulk fuel stocks and equipment.

The MAGTF may require a partial system, complete system or multiple fuel systems. When using a partial system, commanders need to ensure they have adequate equipment to perform the unit's bulk fuel mission. For example, if the mission only requires one tank farm from an AAFS but also has a requirement or possibility for STS operations, the beach unloading assembly must also be taken.

Command Element

The CE, in conjunction with the CSSE, plans and coordinates bulk fuel support for the MAGTF. The CE will coordinate the MAGTF bulk fuel concept with the theater plan to ensure that the MAGTF is prepared to meet any special bulk fuel tasking from the theater commander. Additional tasks for CE could include such things as coordinating area support to other Services.

Normally, the CE will consolidate all the MAGTF fuel requirements and submit them to the appropriate component headquarters or the JTF. Even though daily bulk fuel management is done within the other MAGTF elements, the CE should ensure economy of effort for bulk fuel support. The CE is also responsible for setting the MAGTF bulk fuel stockage objective and for allocation of bulk fuel within the MAGTF. If requirements exceed availability, this is usually done by a bulk petroleum allocation report. See appendix B. The CE will ensure that all bulk fuel reporting requirements established in the OPLANs are met.

Combat Service Support Element

The CSSE is responsible for bulk fuel support and daily management of bulk fuel equipment with the exception of tactical aviation fuel systems. In order for the CSSE to carry out this responsibility, exercises and OPLANs should address procedures and coordination requirements for fuel support in detail. The CSSE then consolidates the requirements and passes them to the CE for sourcing. Depending on the size of the MAGTF and the geographical area, the CE may task the CSSE with sourcing the consolidated requirements with theater agencies. MAGTF elements that receive direct fuel support from the CSSE must coordinate their fuel and support requirements (fuel deliveries, storage, etc.).

Normally, bulk fuel management is the responsibility of CSSE G-3/S-3 and G-4 supply support.

CSSE bulk fuel units can range from a complete bulk fuel company(ies) to a small section, depending on the mission.

Aviation Combat Element

The ACE is responsible for bulk fuel support and daily management of bulk fuel for all tactical aviation fuel systems at the airfields and FARPs. These responsibilities are performed by the ACE G-4/S-4 or within the airfield operations division of the MWSS. The ACE provides bulk fuel support to all organizations within the boundaries of the airfield. This includes support to other Services' aircraft if directed in the theater bulk fuel plan.

For ground equipment fuel support, the ACE is primarily equipped to be self-sufficient. If ground fuel support requirements within the boundaries of an airfield exceed the ACE capabilities, the CSSE should provide any additional support requested.

Bulk fuel sourcing and support procedures for the ACE airfields vary depending on the situation. If the airfields receive bulk fuel directly from theater sources, the CE may task the ACE with coordinating its fuel requirements directly with the theater agency. If the airfield receives fuel support from the CSSE, the ACE will coordinate its fuel requirements directly with the CSSE.

Ground Combat Element

The GCE is primarily a bulk fuel user, not a provider. However, the GCE does have mobile fuel equipment to provide DS to division units. The GCE coordinates fuel support requirements with the CSSE that is providing DS. Normally the GCE will use SIXCONs and mobile refuelers for fuel support to its end users such as tanks and vehicles. If GCE fuel requirements exceed the GCE's fuel support capability, the GCE will request fuel support from the CSSE.

Bulk Fuel Support for the MAGTF

Resupply

The MAGTF bulk fuel distribution system is a push-pull resupply system. Bulk fuel is moved forward (pushed) throughout the MAGTF bulk fuel system based on storage space available and anticipated customer demands. The basic principle is to keep storage tanks full. The customers request (pull) fuel from the bulk fuel system based on their demands. The CE monitors the push and pull sides of the resupply system to ensure fuel movement throughout the system is coordinated with the OPLANs. For example, if a CSSD with a fuel storage system moves to another location, its fuel stocks are drawn down so it can move its equipment. In that case, the CE would not push fuel to the CSSD empty storage. During the drawdown, the CE would ensure continuous fuel support to the units being supported by that CSSD.

Storage

Normally, bulk fuel for MAGTF operations is stored ashore in tactical fuel systems. A bulk fuel company can install and operate four AAFSs with a storage capacity of 4.48 million gallons.

Aircraft are not normally brought ashore until adequate fuel stocks are available. However, refueling operations may commence by relying on afloat storage once the STS pumping rate meets the daily requirement. Another option is to have the aircraft refuel from ships or theater airfields not in the AOA, thus reducing the shore-based requirement.

At issue is the tradeoff between start dates for shore-based air operations and the risk of a fuel cutoff. Any interruption in sea-based fuel support would create a fuel shortage without adequate fuel ashore. Table 5-1, on page 5-6, shows the DOS that four AAFSs can provide to various MAGTFs based on the following assumptions:

- Ground forces consuming fuel at assault rate,
- ACE requiring shore-based fuel, and
- Aircraft sorties being flown at a sustained rate.

Maritime Prepositioning Ships

The rapid offloading and availability of bulk fuel are essential to MPS operations. Notionally, each MPSRON currently carries four AAFS, five TAFDS, and six HERS embarked in 8- by 8- by 20-foot containers. The TFSs are spread-loaded among the various ships so that each ship has a bulk fuel capability. They must be established ashore before the ships can offload their cargo fuel. Therefore, the AAFS and TAFDS are embarked in a manner that allows them to be among the first items of equipment offloaded. MPSs have the capability to carry cargo bulk fuel. Depending on the type of ship, each MPSRON can carry up to 2.5 million gallons of JP-5, and up to 114,000 gallons of motor gasoline (MOGAS).

Fuel Offload

The MPS can offload fuel through a single 6-inch hose line at 600 GPM from a distance of up to 2 miles. The MPS can also offload fuel at pier side or in-stream. At the flow rate of 600 GPM, it takes approximately 36 hours to offload the JP-5, and 5 hours to offload the MOGAS from a single ship. For the offload of both MOGAS and JP-5, separate lines and storage facilities are required. Fuel is pumped ashore through the amphibious bulk liquid transfer system that is

Table 5-1. MAGTF Storage Capability (Gallons).

CSSE				ACE				CSSE/ACE Total Storage
MEF	Unit/TFS System	Qty	Storage Capability	MEF	Unit/TFS System	Qty	Storage Capability	
	Bulk Fuel Company	1	—		MWSS (FW)	2	—	
	AAFS	4	4,480,000		MWSS (RW)	2	—	
	3,000-gal tank	16	48,000		TAFDS	10	3,200,000	
	500-gal bladder	158	79,000		HERS	12	216,000	(MEF) 8,023,000
Total			4,607,000	Total			3,416,000	
MEB	Unit/TFS System	Qty	Storage Capability	MEB	Unit/TFS System	Qty	Storage Capability	
	Bulk Fuel Company	1	—		MWSS (FW)	1	—	
	AAFS	4	4,480,000		MWSS (RW)	1	—	
	3,000-gal tank	4	12,000		TAFDS	7	2,240,000	
	500-gal bladder	56	28,000		HERS	8	144,000	(MEB) 6,904,000
Total			4,520,000	Total			2,384,000	
MEU	Unit/TFS System	Qty	Storage Capability	MEU	Unit/TFS System	Qty	Storage Capability	
	Bulk Fuel Company	1	—		MWSS (RW)			
	AAFS	1	12,000		Fuel Section	1	—	
	3,000-gal tank	2	6,000		HERS	1	18,000	
	500-gal bladder	4	2,000					(MEU) 146,000
Total			128,000	Total			18,000	

Note: Since an MPSRON is designed to support a MEB, the MEB totals were derived from NAVMC 2907, *Maritime Prepositioning Force (MPF) Prepositioning Objective* (19 Dec 00), and current allowances submitted to Total Force Structure.

carried aboard the MPS. The system consists of 10,000 feet of 6-inch diameter hose mounted on a powered hose reel. For installation, the hose reel is loaded on a landing craft utility or a side-loadable warping tug and is normally installed from the beach to the ship. The shore end of the hose is connected to the AAFS with the beach interface unit supplied by the amphibious construction battalion. Under favorable conditions, the hose line system can be installed in 8 to 10 hours and retrieved in 10 to 16 hours.

Unloading Fuel Systems

Early unloading of the fuel systems allows for installation to begin while the rest of the equipment is being offloaded. All fuel-consuming equipment being offloaded should be filled on the ships before offload. This will reduce the immediate need for shore-based fuel support. Mobile refuelers should also be filled before offloading so they can provide required fuel support ashore. Once the ship has offloaded its cargo, it can then be positioned to deploy the hose reel and offload its cargo fuel to the AAFS. In the time it takes to offload the equipment from the ship and deploy the hose reel, the AAFS installation should be to the point that it can start receiving fuel. During site selection for MPSs, operations planners need to consider terrain requirements and locations for the bulk fuel systems and the STS fuel transfer.

Bulk Fuel Reports

Bulk fuel reporting requirements and procedures will vary depending on the exercise and/or operation. Appendices B and C are examples of bulk fuel reports that may be required of the MAGTF in a joint environment. The example in appendix B is from the defense message system.

CHAPTER 6. BULK FUEL INVENTORY MANAGEMENT

The management of fuel inventories involves a full range of actions associated with orders/requisitions, receipt, transfer, issue, and storage of fuel. Bulk fuel support must be planned so product quantities are maintained to support planned operations. The major objectives of an inventory management program are to—

- Ensure all orders, receipts, transfers, issues, losses, gains, and adjustments are properly documented.
- Maintain accountable records on all products.
- Ensure an audit trail of fuel transactions is performed.
- Maintain control over the physical environment to ensure proper product storage can take place with minimal losses.
- Ensure fuel losses are held to a minimum.

References

The requirements and procedures for the accountability of petroleum products are in DOD Manual 4140.25-M. This reference provides policy and guidance for the accountability of petroleum products by Marine Corps activities.

Regardless of the type of fuel equipment being used, units must maintain accounting procedures and records as accurately as possible. This applies to tactical situations using mobile refueling equipment and TFSs. Accounting for fuel in fixed facilities and commercial mobile equipment must be fairly accurate. However, when bulk fuel units perform a physical inventory for TFSs, the physical inventory becomes more difficult and less accurate due to the use of collapsible tanks and miles of tactical hose that may be employed. The key to more accurate accounting for TFSs is for commanders to ensure that local bulk fuel standing operating procedures (SOPs) address unit procedures and requirements for fuel accountability when using TFSs.

Procedures

DOD fuel is purchased and owned at the wholesale level by DESC for direct delivery to the customer. When the Service orders and receives fuel from a defense fuel supply point or a DESC contract, a "sale" may take place if the fuel is transferred to single-user unit. If the fuel is transferred to a multi-user unit and that unit or site holds DESC-owned (capitalized) fuel, a "sale" takes place once the fuel is issued into the individual piece of equipment or aircraft.

Whether a Service is holding wholesale or retail bulk fuel stocks, certain rules of accounting apply to all Services. All bulk fuel holding activities should maintain a property book or logbook inventory record and a physical inventory record. Property book records are an administrative (checkbook) record of all receipts, transfers, and issues, and provide an estimate of the fuel inventory on hand. They are maintained on a daily basis. Physical inventory is a physical measurement of the actual fuel on hand using volume correction to 60 degrees Fahrenheit (F). A physical inventory is conducted periodically (daily, weekly, monthly) depending on the situation. If the differences between the property book records and the physical inventory exceeds the allowable loss/gain, it must be reported through the chain of command.

Fuel Accountability

As with all supplies, the commander considers the accountability of bulk fuel essential. Commanders are also aware that procedures and requirements for bulk fuel accountability will vary depending on the operation, the type of fuel equipment being used, and the situation; for example, combat, training exercise or joint operation. To ensure proper and sound accounting procedures are being followed, the commander and staff need to ensure that accounting procedures are contained in OPLANs and exercise letters of instruction.

However, due to the nature of fuel, certain losses will occur as a result of evaporation, transportation, storage, and handling. Allowable tolerances have been established for these losses and gains by the American Petroleum Institute (API) and adopted by the DOD. There are many variables involved in accounting procedures. The following procedures are common and apply to all bulk fuel operations:

- Access to all bulk fuel stocks must be controlled.
- The quantity and quality of fuel receipts should be validated prior to off-loading.

- The unit of measurement for all fuel receipts is the US gallon corrected for volume to 60 degrees F.
- Discrepancies in excess of allowable losses/gains must be documented and reported.
- Only authorized personnel should make fuel issues.

Reports

Status reports; daily, weekly, monthly fuels issue reports; and monthly bulk fuel accounting summaries are used to maintain accountability of bulk fuel receipts, issues, and stocks on hand. Report content should include the following:

- Opening and closing balances.
- Total issues.
- Total receipts.
- Physical inventory.
- Property book inventory.
- Losses/gains.
- Other applicable information regarding accounting or operational capability.

Daily status reports, including the bulk petroleum contingency report (REPOL), are done per the local commander's SOP. See appendix C for a REPOL example.

CHAPTER 7. BULK FUEL QUALITY SURVEILLANCE PROGRAM

Quality surveillance is the process of determining and maintaining the quality of petroleum and related products to ensure these products are suitable for their intended use. The quality of petroleum products is controlled at origin by the DESC. After receipt of the petroleum products, each Service is responsible for continued surveillance to maintain the quality of petroleum products.

To meet specifications set by DOD, petroleum products undergo quality surveillance from time of purchase until used. The JPO, responsible to the JFC, ensures there is a quality surveillance program within the command and monitors and assists Service components in this program. The theater Army command is responsible for setting up and maintaining a quality surveillance program to support theater Army users. Each Service component is responsible for establishing and maintaining a quality surveillance program for Service-held petroleum stocks.

A vigilant quality surveillance program implemented by properly trained personnel is necessary to protect the original product quality. The fuel systems of modern aircraft and ground vehicles will not function properly if fuel is contaminated with dirt, water, other fuel, or any foreign matter. Actions will be taken to ensure that the product conforms to established technical specifications. These actions include preventive maintenance of equipment; mandatory use of filter separators for aviation fuels (also highly recommended for ground fuels); daily recirculation and visual examination of the product; proper storage, handling, and drainage of water bottoms; and monitoring proper concentrations of additives. The DOD-MIL-STD 3004A and NAVAIR 00-80T-109 are the approved references for quality surveillance.

Personnel

The bulk fuel officer (military occupational specialty [MOS] 1390) or the bulk fuel staff noncommissioned officer (MOS 1391) is responsible for establishing procedures that will ensure the quality of bulk fuel products that are stored and issued. All fuel handling personnel are responsible for following established procedures and ensuring they take the required steps to deliver clean fuel to vehicles and aircraft.

An effective quality surveillance program requires properly trained personnel. Every Marine involved in handling petroleum should be suitably trained in quality control. The activity having physical possession of a product is responsible for quality surveillance.

Specifications

Various types of fuel have critical properties and requirements that must be maintained. Tests determine a product's physical and chemical properties. Each petroleum product has a specification that lists chemical and physical requirements of the fuel. The specifications listed in tables 7-1 and 7-2 on page 7-2 are common government-owned fuels in use by the military today.

Table 7-1. Aviation Fuel Specifications.

AVIATION FUELS	JP-4	JP-5	JET A	JET A-1	JET B	JP-8	100/130
DOD-MIL-SPEC	MIL-DTL-5624T	MIL-DTL-5624T	ASTM-D-1655-04	ASTM-D-1655-04	ASTM-D-1655-04	MIL-DTL-83133E	MIL-G-5572
NSN	9130-00-256-8613	9130-00-273-2379	9130-00-359-2026	9130-00-753-5026	9130-00-111-7350	9130-00-131-5816	9130-00-179-1122
Density (lb/gal)	6.4	6.8	6.8	6.7	6.4	6.7	6.0
Flashpoint (°F)	-20	140	100	100	-20	100	-25
Freeze point (°F)	-72	-51	-40	-53	-58	-53	-76
API gravity (max)	57.0	48.0	51.0	51.0	57.0	51.0	—
API gravity (min)	45.0	36.0	37.0	37.0	45.0	37.0	—
NATO/ASCC symbol	F-40	F-44	F-35	F-34	F-40	F-34	F-18
Specific gravity (typical)	0.769	0.817	0.817	0.805	0.769	0.805	0.703
Vapor pressure (psi)	2.0 to 3.0	—	—	2.0 to 3.0	—	3.0 max	—
Viscosity at -40°C	3.6 cSt	16.5 cSt	15 cSt	15 cSt	3.6 cSt	15 cSt	1.2 cSt
BTU per gal (min)	115,000	120,000	119,000	119,000	115,000	119,000	109,000
BTU per lb (min)	18,400	18,300	18,400	18,400	18,400	18,400	18,700
FSII	yes	yes	optional	optional	optional	yes	no
Corrosion inhibitor	yes	yes	permitted	permitted	permitted	yes	optional

Table 7-2. Ground Fuel Specifications.

GROUND FUELS	Motor Gasoline	DF-1	DFM	DF-2
DOD-MIL-SPEC	ASTM D-4814	A-A-52557	MIL-F-16884	A-A-52557
NSN	9130-00-264-6128	9130-00-286-5286	9140-00-273-2377	9140-00-286-5294
Density (lb/gal)	6.2	6.9	7.0	6.9
Flashpoint (°F)	~ -30	100	140	125
Freeze point (°F)	~ -75	~ 41	30	~ 34
API gravity (max)	71	—	—	42
API gravity (min)	47	—	—	33
NATO/ASCC symbol	F46/F49/F50	F-54	F-76	F-54
Cetane number	—	45	45	45
Cloud point °F (max)	—	-60	30	Spec by user
Pour point ° F (max)	—	Spec by user	20	Spec by user
Viscosity (min)	—	1.4 cSt	1.8 cSt	2.0 cSt
Viscosity (max)	—	3.0 cSt	4.5 cSt	4.3 cSt
Sulfur% (max)	0.10	0.5	1.00	0.5
Operating temp range	—	-25 to 32	—	—
Air Force Reference	TO 42	TO 42	TO 42	TO 42

Legend for Table 7-1 and 7-2:

~ = approximately	US Air Force Technical Order (TO) 42, *Security System Data*
ASCC = Air Standardization Coordinating Committee	DOD MIL-SPEC DTL-5624T, *Turbine Fuel, Aviation, Grades JP-4 and JP-5*
BTU = British thermal unit	DOD MIL-SPEC DTL-83133E, *Turbine Fuel, Aviation, Grade JP-8*
C = Celsius	DOD MIL-SPEC G-5572, *Gasoline, Aviation, Grades 80/87, 100/130, 115/145*
cSt = centistokes; the kinematical unit of viscosity	DOD MIL-SPEC A-A-52557, *Fuel Oil, Diesel; For Posts, Camps and Stations*
DFM = diesel fuel marine	DOD MIL-SPEC F-16884, *Fuel, Navy Distillate*
FSII = fuel system icing inhibitor	ASTM-D-1655-04, *Standard Specification for Aviation Turbine Fuels*
lb/gal = pounds per gallon	ASTM-D-4814, *Standard Specifications for Automatic Spark-Ignition Engine Fuel*
NATO = North Atlantic Treaty Organization	
NSN = National Stock Number	
psi = pounds per square inch	

Testing Kits and Methods

Tactical Petroleum Laboratory, Medium

Each TPLM is capable of conducting the full spectrum of fuel testing as required by the Marine Corps.

Aviation Fuel Contamination Test Kit

The aviation fuel contamination test kit is a portable petroleum quality surveillance kit consisting of components and testing equipment capable of determining contamination levels in aviation fuels. The kit has the capability to take in-line samples in tactical fuel systems, mobile refueling equipment, and commercial refueling equipment. The kit can test for specific gravity, free-water, and particulate contamination in aviation fuel samples. The aviation fuel contamination test kit is associated with the TAFDS and AAFS.

B2 Test Kit

The B2 fuel system icing inhibitor (FSII) test kit is utilized to measure the levels of FSII additives in aviation fuels. The kit consist of a refractor viewer, testing glassware, and other assorted accessories all stored in a briefcase with custom-fit foam padding for each component of the kit.

Flashpoint Test Kit

Each type of fuel ignites or flashes at a given temperature. This test is used to determine the temperature a given fuel will ignite in a controlled environment, per MIL-STD 3004-A. This test will determine if a fuel is within specification limits or determine the type of an unknown fuel. The kit is a self-contained unit that provides all the hardware necessary to conduct flashpoint testing in austere environments at expeditionary airfields or forward operating bases.

Combined Contaminated Fuel Detector Kit

The combined contaminated fuel detector kit is a combined portable unit capable of measuring both solid contaminants and free water (undissolved) in aircraft fuel. The maximum allowable limit of solid contamination for Navy and Marine Corps aviation fuel is 2 milligrams per liter. The maximum allowable limit of free water in fuel at aircraft dispensing points is 5 parts per million in accordance with NAVAIR 00-80T-109.

Correlation Testing

Correlation samples are sent to a supporting laboratory once a month to verify the accuracy of local tests.

Daily/Weekly Testing

Fuel units conduct weekly/daily testing using the applicable test equipment and the combined contaminated fuel detector kit. All personnel in the MOS 1391 are qualified to use the test kits.

Deterioration Limits

Bulk fuel deteriorates when subject to long periods of storage. Therefore, it is important that bulk fuel be issued on a first-in, first-out basis or as quality surveillance indicates. Deterioration occurs when one or more characteristics of the product change to a level outside the specification limits. Examples of deterioration are weathering, oxidation, or loss of additives.

Deterioration limits are tolerances established to permit use of products that do not fully meet specifications. When petroleum products do not meet the deterioration limits, quality surveillance personnel report the facts and circumstances and recommend alternative use or disposition to the commanding officer. If appropriate, proposed recovery measures are also reported.

Testing Properties

Knock Values

Knock values indicate whether a fuel will burn uniformly and evenly in a cylinder without pre-ignition or detonation. The knock values are expressed as octane numbers for automotive type engine gasoline and as a combination of octane and performance numbers for aviation gasoline. These values are determined by comparing the knocking tendency of fuel samples to those of standard test fuels of known knock values in a standard test engine. Fuel of inadequate knock value will reduce the power output of all types of engines. If used for more than brief periods, it could cause overheating of the engine, burned or melted pistons and cylinders, and lubrication failure.

Cetane Number

The ignition quality of a diesel fuel, which is based on a scale resembling that of an octane number, is expressed as a cetane number. This number indicates the length of time (ignition lag) between injection of the fuel and combustion. The cetane number requirement varies with the type of diesel engine. Large and slow speed units in stationary installations do not require diesel fuel with cetane ratings above 40. Smaller, high-speed engines (1,000 rotations per minute or more) require fuel of a higher cetane number. In the absence of test engines, cetane numbers are approximated from the calculated cetane index.

Color

Color is primarily used as an aid for identifying fuels such as aviation and automotive gasolines that have characteristic colors. Failure of fuel to meet its color requirement may indicate the possibility of contamination or deterioration. Darkening of the color of jet fuel may indicate the formation of insoluble gums.

Corrosion

Quantitative and qualitative tests for corrosion indicate whether products are free of corrosion tendencies. The quantitative test determines total sulfur content. This is important, particularly when a product is to be burned in lamps, heating appliances, or engines. The qualitative test shows if fuel will corrode the metal parts of fuel systems.

Existent Gum

As the name implies, gum is the sticky, tacky, varnish-like material that is undesirable to have in fuel systems. Existent gum is the nonvolatile residue present in gasoline or jet fuels after they have been tested. The results indicate the quantity of gum deposit that may occur if the product is used immediately but do not indicate the possibility of gum formation when the product is stored. When present in excess, gum clogs fuel lines, filter and pump screens, and carburetor jets; causes manifold deposits and sticky intake valves; and reduces the knock value of gasoline.

Potential Gum

Potential gum (sometimes called oxidation stability) is determined by a test that indicates the presence of gum-forming materials and the relative tendency of gasolines and jet fuels to form gums after a specified period of accelerated aging. This value is used as an indication of the tendency of fuels to form gum during extended storage.

Retention of the original properties of a fuel after prolonged storage is known as the stability of the fuel. When added to fuels, chemical inhibitors retard gum formation but will not reduce gum that has already been formed. The effects of the potential gum are similar to those described for existent gum. Gum may be expressed as the "induction period" (sometimes called the breakdown time). This is a measure of the time in minutes that elapse during the accelerated test until the fuel rapidly absorbs oxygen. For aviation gasoline and jet fuel, the potential gum may be expressed as the potential for accelerated gum. This is the gum plus the lead deposits (from lead fuels) measured at the end of a specified accelerated aging (oxidation) period.

Flashpoint

The flashpoint is the lowest temperature at which vapors rising from a petroleum product (or when exposed to test flame under specified conditions) ignite momentarily (flash) on application. The flashpoint of a petroleum product indicates the fire hazard in handling and storing it. It applies to fuel oils, diesel fuels, JP-5, kerosene, and solvents. It is not used for JP-4. The flashpoint test also indicates the combination of a product. For example, the presence of very small quantities of gasoline will make the flashpoint of a diesel fuel considerably lower than the minimum operating level. The flashpoint of new lubricating oil is used primarily for identification and classification. The flashpoint of the oil must be above the operating temperature of the engine in which it is to be used.

Cloud and Pour Points

The cloud point is the temperature at which wax crystals (normally held in solution or water) in oil separate, causing the oil to appear cloudy or hazy. In wick-fed systems, the wax crystals may clog the wick. Both wax crystals and water may block filter passages in fuel systems. The pour point of oil indicates its behavior at low temperature. The fact that oil has a specific pour point is no guarantee that it can be handled or is a satisfactory lubricant at that temperature.

Distillation

The distillation process is used to measure the volatility of a petroleum product. The lower boiling fractions of gasoline indicate the starting ability of a gasoline engine at a given temperature and the engine's ability to warm up quickly. An excessive amount of highly volatile constituents in gasoline may cause vapor lock. Conversely, a gasoline with an excessive amount of "heavy ends" may not completely burn in the combustion chamber. This may cause damage through excessive dilution of crankcase oil. Specifications designate minimum and maximum percentages of fractions to be evaporated at specified temperatures, as well as initial and final boiling points. A gasoline with a high end point and a high percentage of residues may be contaminated with fuel oils or other oils. A fuel oil with a considerably lower initial boiling point flashpoint than normal may be contaminated with gasoline.

Viscosity

Viscosity is the measure of a liquid's resistance to flow. Specified minimum and maximum flow rates are required for all fuel oils and lubricating oils. A fuel oil's viscosity determines how the oil will flow to the burners, the extent to which it would be atomized, and the temperature at which the oil must be maintained to be atomized properly.

Reid Vapor Pressure

The vapor pressure of a fuel, which indicates the tendency to vaporize, is determined by the Reid vapor test. For any given gasoline, vapor pressure increases with temperature. Gasolines must have a certain vapor pressure to ensure adequate starting and accelerating qualities.

Carbon Residue

The carbon residue test indicates the carbonizing properties of lubricating or burner oil. However, carbon residue from lubricating oils is not directly related to carbon formation in the engine. This test gives an indication of the type of carbon formation (loose or flaky or hard and flinty). It is used primarily as an identify-and-control test in conjunction with other specification tests. After distilling 90 percent of diesel fuel, the carbon remaining in the 10 percent residue must be low enough to avoid carbon deposits. High carbon fuels should be checked carefully for carbon formation.

Bottom Sediment and Water

Petroleum products may gain sediment and water during storage and handling. This can adversely affect the performance of the equipment in which the products are used.

Aviation Fuels

Contamination by bottom sediment and water can often be detected visually. As a general rule, aviation fuel must be clean and bright and contain no free water. The terms clean and bright do not refer to the natural color of the fuel; the various grades of the fuel have dyes added. Jet fuels are not dyed and could be any color from water white to amber. "Clean" means the absence of any cloud, emulsion, readily visible sediment, or entrained water. "Bright" refers to the shiny appearance of clean dry fuels. Clouds, haze, specks of sediment, or entrained water indicate that the fuel is unsuitable, pointing to a breakdown of fuel handling equipment. Steps should

be taken to find the trouble immediately. *NOTE: All the following information is also applicable to automotive fuels.*

Cloudy or Hazy Fuel

Cloudy or hazy fuel usually indicates water, but it may also indicate excessive amounts of fine sediment or finely dispersed stabilized emulsion. Fuel containing either is not acceptable. When clean and bright fuel cools, a light cloud may form indicating that dissolved water has precipitated out. A precipitation cloud represents a very slight amount of fresh water. However, even a slight amount of fresh water is not desirable in aviation fuel. Fuel that shows some precipitation may not be clean and cannot be accepted or used. Filter separator elements should be replaced and water and emulsion should be removed from the source tank. A filter/separator can be used to remove the precipitation by recirculation or by draining the fuel upstream.

Sediment in Fuel

Specks or granules of sediment indicate particles in size range greater than 0.8 microns. An appreciable number of such particles in a sample indicate a failure of the filter/separator, or a dirty sample container. Even with the most efficient filter/separator and careful fuel handling, an occasional visible particle will be noted. The sediment ordinarily noted is an extremely fine powder, rouge, or silt. In a clean sample of fuel, sediment should not be visible. If sediment continues to be noted, appropriate surveillance tests and corrective measures must be applied to the fuel handling systems.

Diesel Fuels and Burner Oils

To avoid fuel pump and injector difficulties, diesel fuels must be clean and should not contain more than a trace of foreign substances. Excessive sediment and rust in burner oils will plug the burner tip, and the fuel will not atomize properly. Water can cause ragged operation and may corrode the fuel handling system. The types of equipment and burner oils will determine the amount of sediment permissible in the fuel.

Lubricating Oils

Care should be taken to avoid contaminating lubricating oils with water. Water will hasten decomposition of many oils, wash out additives, cause the oil to emulsify, and lead to engine failure. In used lubricating oils, sediment and water may have been caused by poor maintenance, failure of screens, or by condensation of combustion products.

Ash

Burning off the organic matter and weighing the remaining inorganic matter determine the ash in oil. Straight mineral oils usually contain a small trace of ash. Oils containing metallic salts as additives will have larger amounts of ash. Increased amounts of ash indicate contamination with inorganic matter such as sand, dust, and rust. Increased ash in straight mineral oils may indicate contamination with additive type oils. The ash in diesel fuels must be very low because any abrasive substances may damage the internal metal surfaces of the engines and may form deposits on working surfaces. Residual fuel oils should also have low amounts of ash to prevent corrosion or embrittlement of fireboxes and boiler tubes.

Foam Stability

All oils will foam to some extent when agitated. The foam that is formed in oils that contain additives is often very stable. Instead of breaking up quickly, the foam tends to build up, and oil is lost through the breather outlets and other openings in the engine crankcase. Therefore, additive-type motor oils are frequently treated with antifoam agents to eliminate potential foam problems. The foam test requires agitating the oil until the foam is formed and then noting the time required for the foam to break up and disappear.

Gravity

Accurate determination of the gravity of petroleum is necessary for converting measured volumes to volumes of the standard temperature of 60 degrees F. Gravity is a factor governing the quality of crude oils. However, the gravity of a petroleum product is an uncertain indication of its quality. Combined with other properties, gravity can be used to give approximate hydrocarbon composition and heat of combustion. The gravity scale most used in the US is the API gravity. A change of gravity may indicate a change of composition caused by mixing grades of products.

Water Reaction

This test determines the presence of water-miscible components in aviation gasolines and turbine fuels, and the effects of these components on the fuel-water interface.

Fuel System Icing Inhibitor Test

This is a quantitative test used to determine the concentration of the FSII in jet fuel. The FSII additive (ethylene glycol monomthyl ether-glycerol) prevents ice formation in aircraft fuel systems. Testing is performed by many methods (such as colormetric, seisor refractometer, freezing point, and titration). The potassium dichromatesulfuric acid titremetric procedure is the method preferred by the Air Force.

Water Separometer Index Modified

The water separometer index modified test measures the ease with which a fuel releases dispersed or emulsified water. Fuels having a low water separometer index modified rating will prevent filter/separators from functioning properly.

Particulate Contaminant

Excessive sediment will clog fuel lines and internal fuel filters on aircraft. Sediment may also cause wear on metal parts and, when burned, may form deposits causing premature engine failure. The two tests for particulate contaminant in aviation turbine fuels are the Millipore test and the color comparison standards test (the Air Force method).

Undissolved Water

Undissolved (free) water in aviation fuels can encourage the growth of microorganisms and subsequent corrosion in aircraft tanks. It can also lead to icing of filters in the fuel system. Free water is controlled in ground fueling equipment by filter/separators. The Aqua-Glo test is a quick and accurate way to determine the amount of free water in liquid petroleum products. The procedure is found in ASTM D-3240-91 (2001), *Standard Test Method for Undissolved Water in Aviation Turbine Fuels*. Water in fuel can cause the following severe problems:

- Corrosion of tanks, equipment, and lines due to the formation of hydrogen sulfide, an extremely corrosive compound.
- Removal of FSII from aviation turbine fuels.
- Clogging of fuel lines and filters, particularly at high altitudes.
- Support of microbiotic growth sometimes found in water and fuel interface in jet tanks.

Reclamation

Reclamation is the process of restoring or changing the quality of an unsuitable product to meet quality assurance specifications. Fuel can be reclaimed for use by downgrading, blending, purifying, or removing water. Captured fuel should be exploited whenever possible to reduce the logistical burden, but only after testing is performed by a qualified person. The intended use of captured fuel will dictate the extent of testing.

Fuel that cannot be used for its intended purpose may be used as a lower grade of the same or similar product if it meets that product's specifications.

The most common causes of off-specification fuel are contamination and deterioration. Contamination occurs when one or more grades or types of products are inadvertently mixed, or a product contains foreign matter such as dirt, dust, rust, water, or emulsions. Once a product has been identified as being off-specification, the following reclamation procedures can be taken:

- **Downgrading.** Approval for an off-specification or contaminated product for other than its intended use.
- **Blending.** Predetermined quantities of two or more similar products are mixed to produce a petroleum product or intermediate grade or quality.
- **Purification.** The removal of contaminating agents by filtration or dehydration.
- **Dehydration.** The removal of water by a filtering or settling process. Water in most light products will settle out if allowed to stand undisturbed for 12 to 24 hours.
- **Inhibiting.** Adding or restoring additives.
- **Disposal.** As per local SOP.

PART II. BULK WATER OPERATIONS

CHAPTER 8. FUNDAMENTALS

Potable water supply has always been a critical factor on the battlefield. A lack of water can demoralize and debilitate personnel. Three of the four major causes of death in the Civil War were due to contaminated water. With the discovery of bacteria, scientists began to understand that contaminated water caused diseases and infected wounds. A lack of water can also determine the outcome of a war. In 1915, the British commander at Gallipoli, Lieutenant General Sir Frederick Stopford, and his commander, who were actively involved in the landing at Suvla Bay, believed that the shortage of water was the major cause for their failure to take the heights before the Turks occupied them in force.

Improvements to Water Support

The Marine Corps is constantly seeking to improve its water support capability to meet the needs of the Marine Corps and if necessary, the needs of other Services. Consumption factors have been developed to assist in planning for adequate water support and new equipment has been developed to purify all sources of water, to include nuclear, biological, and chemical (NBC) contaminated water. Through the latest technology, quality, and expedient training, the bulk water units are better prepared to provide Marines a most valuable commodity—water.

Concept of Bulk Water Operations

The basic concept of bulk water support is to source or produce water as close to the user as possible. This requires proper planning of the water point selection for bulk water, if required, and purification, storage, and distribution of bulk water.

Bulk Water Support Responsibility

Bulk water support is normally a Service responsibility. However, during joint operations, the JFC may assign the responsibility for water support based on the predominant user concept. This means that the greatest volume user in an area would provide bulk water support above and beyond the organic Service capabilities to all forces operating in the area. The actual procedures used to provide bulk water support to the Services will depend on conditions in the AO.

Deployments

In most deployments, Marine Corps forces will be capable of partial or complete water self-sufficiency using organic water equipment and HN or commercial support. In geographic regions with adequate surface water resources, the commander is likely to establish multiple water points in the vicinity of his forces.

Production and Storage

The production of water is the purification of existing water sources into potable water. The extent to which a water point is developed depends primarily on the time, materials, and the personnel available to do the work. Water storage should be sufficient to meet the daily demands and allow water production to continue. Having adequate water storage avoids frequent time-consuming start-ups and shutdowns of the water production equipment.

Distribution

In most situations, water distribution is the weak link of the water support system. Getting water from the production and storage sites to the user can be equipment and manpower intensive. Water should be produced as close to the end user as possible. Marine forces must make efficient use of all available assets in conducting water distribution operations. Getting water from the storage site to the using units can involve utilizing all organic water distribution assets.

CHAPTER 9. WATER EQUIPMENT

Marine Corps water equipment has to meet a wide range of requirements, from providing support for near shore operations to supporting inland operations. To meet these requirements, the Marine Corps has developed various water equipment end items and the family of water supply support equipment. USMC equipment has the capability to purify both freshwater and saltwater. However, the Marine Corps does not have an organic well drilling capability. The MAGTF must be augmented by elements from the naval construction force in order to have this capability.

Water Equipment End Items

Shower Unit

The shower unit (TAMCN B0055) consists of six separate, identical, and interchangeable shower modules with interconnecting hoses, electric feed water and drain pumps, and a drain hose. The unit has a self-contained, oil-fired boiler water heater capable of providing 120-degree F water at a rate of 20 GPM.

Field Laundry Unit

The bare base laundry facility is a pallet-mounted, self-contained unit consisting of an electrical panel, washer, extractor, dryer, air compressor, water pump, clothes bin, and water heater. Those components are mounted on two platforms, which have 463L pallet locking rail assemblies. The M-80 water heater, supplied with the laundry unit, is a self-contained fuel-fired assembly capable of providing 120-degree F water at a rate of 20 GPM. The laundry unit provides the capability to launder fabrics worn by individual Marines and organizational items with a maximum output of 120 pounds per hour.

Reverse Osmosis Water Purification Unit

The reverse osmosis water purification unit (ROWPU) is an ISO frame-mounted, portable water purification system capable of purifying almost any type of water, to include freshwater, brackish water, and saltwater. The ROWPU is capable of removing NBC contaminants, minerals, and biological impurities. The single greatest benefit of the reverse osmosis process is the ability to desalinate seawater. The ROWPU is powered by a 30-kilowatt generator set and is capable of producing potable water at a rate of 600 GPH.

Tactical Water Purification System

The tactical water purification system (TWPS) will replace the aging 600-GPH ROWPU at a 1:2 ratio. The TWPS is a fully contained, skid-mounted water purification system capable of purifying, storing, and dispensing water meeting Tri-Service Field Water Quality Standards for long-term consumption. The TWPS is powered by a 60-kilowatt generator set and is capable of producing up to 1,500 GPH of potable water in an expeditionary environment. The TWPS can purify a broad range of water sources, to include freshwater, brackish water, and saltwater. It can also purify water that has been exposed to NBC warfare agents. The TWPS has five extended capabilities modules packaged separately in reusable boxes:

- Cold weather module.
- Supplemental module.
- Ocean intake structure system module.
- NBC water treatment module.
- NBC survivability module.

Medium Freshwater Purification Unit

The medium freshwater purification unit (LMT 3000) is a portable, self-contained water purification unit for purifying turbid and bacteria polluted freshwater. It provides a method of producing potable water at the rate of 1,500 to 3,000 GPH. The system contains all functional apparatus and supplies to process approximately 20,000 gallons of potable water per day once the user has a water source and storage capability.

Water Quality Analysis Set-Purification

The water quality analysis set-purification (WQAS-P) consists of the equipment necessary for testing water quality. It is self-contained in a portable, waterproof suitcase. The WQAS-P is used to test total dissolved solids, oxygen reduction potential, pH, chlorine, conductivity, resistivity, turbidity, and temperature. These factors determine if a raw water source is suitable for use and they impact the efficiency of the water purification equipment. The digital technology used assigns a numeric value to each item tested so that different water sources can be compared to see which is better in terms of water quality. The WQAS-P may also contain the optional M272 chemical agents water testing kit.

M149 Water Trailer

The M149 water trailer can transport 400 gallons of potable and non-potable water over highways and cross-country terrain. The water tank is constructed of stainless steel with double walls. Two inches of urethane foam is used as insulation between the walls. It is equipped with four dispensing faucets and one drain faucet. A manhole is located on the top of the water tank for filling and cleaning. The trailer is also equipped with a bracket at the manhole to allow for heating of the water with the standard M67 immersion heater. The trailer can be towed on highways at 50 miles per hour and cross-country at 30 miles per hour by a 2-1/2 ton vehicle or larger.

SIXCON Water Pump Module

The SIXCON water pump module is a component of the SIXCON system—a module system consisting of five tank modules and one pump module. The six modules attach together to form an ISO/American National Standards Institute configured 8- by 8- by 20-foot module. The SIXCON water pump module has the capability for dispensing potable and non-potable water. It has a 125 GPM pumping rate and includes ancillary components for two dispensing points. It is used with the SIXCON water storage module. The SIXCON water modules can be used as a mobile water-dispensing asset or as a stationary dispensing capability.

SIXCON Water Storage Module

The SIXCON water storage module is a component of the SIXCON system—a module system consisting of five tank modules and one pump module. The six modules attach together to form an ISO/American National Standards Institute configured 8- by 8- by 20-foot module. The SIXCON water storage module is a stainless steel tank encased within the module frame and has a capacity of 900 gallons. The water tank is covered with at least 1 inch of foam insulation to keep stored water from freezing or heating up. It has the ancillary components necessary for interconnecting to other SIXCON water storage modules and the SIXCON water pump module (USMC TAMCN B1581). The SIXCON water modules can be used as a mobile water-dispensing asset or as a stationary dispensing capability.

Family of Water Supply Support Equipment

To provide flexible and responsive water support, the Marine Corps has developed a family of water supply support equipment (WSSE). Each system is designed and configured specifically to support a unique mission using similar components. The ability to alter fundamental system configurations and the interchangeability of components allow the creation of limitless combinations of tailored systems to meet mission requirements. The family of WSSE consists of 22 TAMCNs. Current allowances of these items can be found in the unit's table of organization and equipment.

500-Gallon Collapsible Potable Water Drum

The 500-gallon collapsible potable water drum is a durable, non-vented, hermetically sealed, collapsible fabric container of four-ply construction used to store and transport potable water. When filled to its 500-gallon capacity, the drum is cylindrical in shape and can be towed and lifted by means of a towing and lifting yoke (USMC TAMCN B2730). The 500-gallon collapsible potable water drum is used with the forward area water point supply system (FAWPSS) (TAMCN B0676).

3,000-Gallon Collapsible Fabric Water Tank

The 3,000-gallon collapsible fabric water tank is used for storage of potable and non-potable water in support of WSSE, tactical water purification systems, and general water storage. It is constructed of impregnated fabric and designed for quick setup/teardown. The tank is equipped with a removable cover, flotation ring, repair kit, ground cloth, and two 2-inch valves.

20,000-Gallon Collapsible Water Tank

The 20,000-gallon collapsible water tank is constructed of impregnated fabric and equipped with 4-inch elbow hose connections for storage, receipt, and issue of bulk water. The 20,000-gallon collapsible water tank assembly includes an aluminum tank chest, ground cloth, emergency repair kit, and required components for venting and draining.

50,000-Gallon Collapsible Water Tank

The 50,000-gallon collapsible water tank is constructed of impregnated fabric and equipped with 4-inch elbow hose connections for storage, receipt, and issue of bulk water. The 50,000-gallon collapsible water tank assembly includes an aluminum tank chest, ground cloth, emergency repair kit, and required components for venting and draining.

Forward Area Water Point Supply System

The FAWPSS is a portable, self-contained water dispensing system for potable water. It consists of a 125-GPM pump, hoses, and ancillary components necessary to establish four distribution points. The FAWPSS is used in conjunction with the 500-gallon collapsible potable water drum (USMC TAMCN B0571).

Hypochlorination Unit, Purification

The hypochlorination unit, purification provides the capability to chlorinate water to levels acceptable for consumption. It is designed to mix a proportional amount of hypochlorite solution (sanitizing agent) with water in the tactical water distribution system (TWDS). The unit may be positioned in the TWDS so that water is chlorinated prior to entering the storage tank or before delivery to the user. It is skid-mounted and designed to operate at 2 to 100 GPM. It is associated with the TWDS and tank farm interconnection sets.

350-GPM Water Pump

The 350-GPM water pump assembly is designed specifically to transfer water, and is the primary pump within the water supply tank farm. It consists of an air-cooled, three-cylinder diesel engine and a self-priming centrifugal pump mounted on a two-wheel frame assembly. The pump has an output volume of 350 GPM and a designed working pressure of 125 psi. It is used in the 350-GPM pump tank farm interconnection set (USMC TAMCN B2138).

125-GPM Pump Set

The 125-GPM pump set is a compact, frame-mounted, general purpose pump. It is comprised of a centrifugal pump, diesel engine, and ancillary hoses. The pump set is used in conjunction with the TWDS, tank farm interconnection sets, or as a general use pump.

Tank Farm Interconnection Set, Dual Tank

The tank farm interconnection set, dual tank is designed to interconnect two 50,000-gallon (USMC TAMCN 2630) and/or two 20,000-gallon (USMC TAMCN 2631) collapsible storage tanks. The kit consists of 4-inch hoses, valves, and connectors necessary to interconnect the collapsible water storage tanks within the water supply tank farm.

Tank Farm Interconnection Set, Bag Filler

The tank farm interconnection set, bag filler is used to provide an alternative distribution point within the water supply tank farms. The kit consists of various size hoses, valves, nozzles, and connectors necessary to connect the alternate distribution point to the water supply tank farm.

Tank Farm Interconnection Set, 4-inch Hose

The tank farm interconnection set, 4-inch hose is designed to provide the medium to high volume discharge point from the water supply support tank farm. The set contains 4-inch hoses, valves, couplings, and assorted hardware.

Tank Farm Interconnection Set, 2-inch Hose

The tank farm interconnection set, 2-inch hose is designed to provide the low to medium volume distribution points from the water supply tank farm. The set contains 2-inch hoses, valves, couplings, and assorted hardware.

Tank Farm Interconnection Set, 4-inch Discharge Hose

The tank farm hose interconnection set, 4-inch discharge hose provides the two crossover hose lines for the water supply tank farm. The kit contains all required 4-inch hoses, tees, couplings, and hardware for either input or discharge to other WSSE systems.

Tank Farm Interconnection Set, Hose Nozzle

The tank farm interconnection set, hose nozzle provides the low volume, hand held nozzle discharge points for the water supply tank farm. The kit contains the required 4-, 2-, and 1 1/2-inch hoses, valves, reducers, couplings, nozzles, and nozzle stands for installation.

Tank Farm Interconnection Set, Accessory Kit

The tank farm interconnection set, accessory kit is designed to aid in overall water supply tank farm connection. The kit contains 4-, 2-, and 1 1/2-inch hoses; groove clamped pipe system; threaded and cam-lock type adapters; required valves; and associated hardware.

Tank Farm Interconnection Set, 350-GPM Pump

The tank farm interconnection set, 350-GPM pump provides the means to connect the main 350-GPM pump into the water supply tank farm. The kit contains 4-inch hoses, valves, couplings, and associated hardware. Also included is an adapter used to connect the hypochlorination unit (USMC TAMCN B1140) into the system.

Tank Farm Interconnection Set, 125-GPM Pump

The tank farm interconnection set, 125-GPM pump is designed to install the auxiliary 125-GPM pump into the water supply tank farm. The kit contains 2-inch hoses, reducers, valves, and associated couplings.

Tactical Water Distribution System, Pump Station

The TWDS, pump station provides the components and couplings necessary to connect the 600-GPM water pump (USMC TAMCN 2394) within the TWDS. Each pump station contains couplings, valves, components, and 6-inch hoses for installation of the 600-GPM pump.

Tactical Water Distribution System, Storage Assembly

The TWDS, storage assembly is designed to provide an in-line storage and distribution capability when used in conjunction with the TWDS distribution point assembly (USMC TAMCN B2393), and the collapsible 20,000- and 50,000-gallon collapsible water storage tanks (USMC TAMCN B2631 and B2632). Each storage assembly contains the necessary couplings, valves, components, and 6-inch hoses for interconnecting the TWDS distribution point and storage assemblies.

Tactical Water Distribution System, Distribution Point Assembly

The TWDS, distribution point assembly provides the capability for two distribution points within the TWDS system. The TWDS distribution point assembly contains the necessary couplings, valves, components, and hoses to connect two distribution points to the various TWDS assemblies.

Tactical Water Distribution System, 600-GPM Pumping Assembly

The TWDS, 600-GPM pumping assembly is designed specifically to transfer potable water, and is the primary pump within the TWDS. It consists of a water-cooled, four-cylinder diesel engine and a self-priming centrifugal pump mounted on a two-wheel frame assembly. The pump has an output volume of 600 GPM at 350 feet of head and a designed working pressure of 125 psi.

Tactical Water Distribution System, 5-Mile Segment Assembly

The TWDS, 5-mile segment assembly provides the capability to transfer bulk water over distances up to 5 miles. The assembly contains the 6-inch lightweight lay-flat hose in 500-foot sections, flaking boxes for employment and retrieval of hose, hose repair kit, evacuation and displacement kit, roadway crossing guards, hose line suspension kit, and ancillary components necessary for employment of the 6-inch hose line.

CHAPTER 10. WATER SUPPORT PLANNING

The key to successful water support is innovative and flexible planning. Planning for water support may range from a MAGTF contingency operation in areas without a pre-established water support base to an operation involved in allied/HN support where water support is partially supplied. For contingency operations, water planners must ensure that water units are structured to allow situation-dependent growth and maturity. This flexibility is a key to the MAGTF commander's ability to support the operation.

Water support planning is a continual process that involves the matching of an operational scenario to prepositioned supplies and equipment. Planning for water support must ensure that the MAGTF can perform its mission in the time required. Water support units and equipment need to be time-phased in the AO so that water support and preventive medicine units arrive on time to provide adequate and continuous water support during an operation.

Planning Guidance

Water planners at all levels must include water supply procedures and guidance in exercise and operation plans. The water supply procedures are set forth in Army Field Manual (FM) 10-52, *Water Supply in Theaters of Operations*; FM 10-52-1, *Water Supply Point Equipment and Operations*; Navy Medical Command Publication (NAVMED) P-5010-5, *Preventive Medicine Manual (Navy)* or in Army Technical Bulletin Medical (TB MED) 577, *Occupational and Environmental Health: Sanitary Control and Surveillance of Field Water Supplies*. Planners also need to ensure that the force structure has adequate resources for water production, storage, and distribution.

Water support planning is a continual process that begins with the identification of the force size and planned deployment rate. Time-phased water requirements are then determined and units are selected and scheduled for deployment based on the requirements.

Some specific areas that are critical to effective water support planning are as follows:

- Development of detailed water production, storage, and distribution plan.
- Identification of water support requirements for other Services, allied forces, or HN labor forces, as directed.
- Water quality procedures.

Water Requirements

Planning for water support begins with determining water requirements. Water requirements will depend upon the environment, the tactical situation, and the size of the force. Water requirements are flexible. They may not be the same each day. Some requirements, such as cooking, may be indefinite while others may only be for a specific period of time.

Consumption Requirements

A number of water consumption requirements are based on the size of the force. These may include but are not limited to the following:

- Drinking.
- Field feeding.
- Heat casualty treatment.
- Laundering.
- Centralized hygiene.
- Personal hygiene.
- Level-1 medical treatment.
- Level-2 medical treatment.

- NBC decontamination.
- Engineer construction.
- Vehicle maintenance.
- Aircraft maintenance.

Region

Water consumption depends on the region. For specific regional requirements, see tables 10-1 through 10-4.

Requirements Determination

A number of computations must be made to determine supply, purification, and storage requirements for water.

Supply Requirement

To compute the total daily water requirement of the force, multiply the actual personnel strength by the proper consumption factor. The total, expressed as gallons per day, includes 10 percent for evaporation and waste loss.

Purification Requirement

The amount of purification equipment to support the daily requirement has to be determined. To do this, divide the total daily requirement by the daily production capability of one purification unit. Under normal conditions, water purification equipment is operated 24 hours per day. However, many other factors affect the water production. Planners should coordinate with the equipment operators to get an accurate estimate of the water production capability.

Storage Requirement

Temperate and tropical regions usually do not require large amounts of water to be stored. In arid regions, large quantities of potable water must be stored. The storage requirement is based on resupply times, daily requirements, and the DOS requirement established by the MAGTF commander.

Essential Consumption

When enough potable water cannot be produced to meet all the requirements, all but essential consumption must be reduced. Essential water requirements include drinking, personal hygiene, field feeding, medical treatment, heat casualty treatment, and, in arid regions, vehicle and aircraft maintenance. Consumption rates under these conditions are classified as "minimum," enough for a force to survive up to 1 week. Requirements exceeding 1 week are classified as "sustaining." In this classification, nonessential consumption includes that for centralized hygiene, laundry, and construction.

Table 10-1. Water Requirements for Temperate Zones.

Company	Daily Gallons-Per-Man Requirements	
Function	Sustaining	Minimum
Drinking	1.5	1.5
Personal Hygiene	1.7	0.3
Field Feeding	1.3	0.8
SUBTOTAL	4.5	2.6
+ 10% WASTE	0.5	0.3
TOTAL	5.0	2.9
Regimental Landing Team	**Daily Gallons-Per-Man Requirements**	
Function	Sustaining	Minimum
Drinking	1.5	1.5
Personal Hygiene	1.7	1
Field Feeding	2.8	0.8
Medical Treatment	0.4	0.4
SUBTOTAL	6.4	3.7
+ 10% WASTE	0.6	0.4
TOTAL	7	4.1
Battalion	**Daily Gallons-Per-Man Requirements**	
Function	Sustaining	Minimum
Drinking	1.5	1.5
Personal Hygiene	1.7	1
Field Feeding	2.8	0.8
SUBTOTAL	6	3.3
+ 10% WASTE	0.6	0.3
TOTAL	6.6	3.6
MEF	**Daily Gallons-Per-Man Requirements**	
Function	Sustaining	Minimum
Drinking	1.5	1.5
Personal Hygiene	1.7	1
Field Feeding	2.8	0.8
Level-1 Medical Treatment	0.4	0.4
Level-2 Medical Treatment	0.7	0.7
SUBTOTAL	7.1	4.4
+ 10% WASTE	0.7	0.4
TOTAL	7.8	4.8

Table 10-2. Water Requirements for Tropical Zones.

Company	Daily Gallons-Per-Man Requirements	
Function	Sustaining	Minimum
Drinking	3.0	3.0
Personal Hygiene	1.7	0.3
Field Feeding	1.3	0.8
Heat Casualty Treatment	0.2	0.2
Subtotal	6.2	4.3
+10% Waste	0.6	0.4
Total	6.8	4.7
Regimental Landing Team	**Daily Gallons-Per-Man Requirements**	
Function	Sustaining	Minimum
Drinking	3.0	3.0
Personal Hygiene	1.7	1.0
Field Feeding	2.8	0.8
Heat Casualty Treatment	0.2	0.2
Medical Treatment	0.4	0.4
Subtotal	8.1	5.4
+10% Waste	0.8	0.5
Total	8.9	5.9
Battalion	**Daily Gallons-Per-Man Requirements**	
Function	Sustaining	Minimum
Drinking	3.0	3.0
Personal Hygiene	1.7	1.0
Field Feeding	2.8	0.8
Heat Casualty Treatment	0.2	0.2
Subtotal	7.7	5.0
+10% Waste	0.8	0.5
Total	8.5	5.5
MEF	**Daily Gallons-Per-Man Requirements**	
Function	Sustaining	Minimum
Drinking	3.0	3.0
Personal Hygiene	1.7	1.0
Field Feeding	2.8	0.8
Heat Casualty Treatment	0.2	0.2
Level-1 Medical Treatment	0.4	0.4
Level-2 Medical Treatment	0.9	0.9
Subtotal	9.0	6.3
+10% Waste	0.9	0.6
Total	9.9	6.9

Table 10-3. Water Requirements for Arctic Zones.

Company	Daily Gallons-Per-Man Requirements	
Function	Sustaining	Minimum
Drinking	2.0	2.0
Personal Hygiene	1.7	0.3
Field Feeding	1.3	0.8
Subtotal	7.5	3.1
+10% Waste	0.8	0.3
Total	8.3	3.4
Regimental Landing Team	Daily Gallons-Per-Man Requirements	
Function	Sustaining	Minimum
Drinking	2.0	2.0
Personal Hygiene	1.7	1.0
Field Feeding	2.8	0.8
Medical Treatment	0.4	0.4
Subtotal	6.9	4.2
+10% Waste	0.7	0.4
Total	7.6	4.6
Battalion	Daily Gallons-Per-Man Requirements	
Function	Sustaining	Minimum
Drinking	2.0	2.0
Personal Hygiene	1.7	1.0
Field Feeding	2.8	0.8
Subtotal	6.5	3.8
+10% Waste	0.7	0.4
Total	7.2	4.2
MEF	Daily Gallons-Per-Man Requirements	
Function	Sustaining	Minimum
Drinking	2.0	2.0
Personal Hygiene	1.7	1.0
Field Feeding	2.8	0.8
Level-1 Medical Treatment	0.4	0.4
Level-2 Medical Treatment	0.7	0.7
Subtotal	7.6	4.9
+10% Waste	0.8	0.5
Total	8.4	5.4

Table 10-4. Water Requirements for Arid Zones.

Company	Daily Gallons-Per-Man Requirements	
Function	Sustaining	Minimum
Drinking	3.0	3.0
Personal Hygiene	1.7	0.3
Field Feeding	1.3	0.8
Heat Casualty Treatment	0.2	0.2
Vehicle Maintenance	0.2	0.2
Subtotal	6.4	4.5
+10% Waste	0.6	0.5
Total	7.5	5.0
Regimental Landing Team	Daily Gallons-Per-Man Requirements	
Function	Sustaining	Minimum
Drinking	3.0	3.0
Personal Hygiene	1.7	1.0
Field Feeding	2.8	0.8
Heat Casualty Treatment	0.2	0.2
Vehicle Maintenance	0.2	0.2
Medical Treatment	0.4	0.4
Centralized Hygiene	1.8	0.0
Construction	0.5	0.0
Aircraft Maintenance	0.2	0.2
Subtotal	10.8	5.8
+10% Waste	1.1	0.6
Total	11.9	6.4
Battalion	Daily Gallons-Per-Man Requirements	
Function	Sustaining	Minimum
Drinking	3.0	3.0
Personal Hygiene	1.7	1.0
Field Feeding	2.8	0.8
Heat Casualty Treatment	0.2	0.2
Vehicle Maintenance	0.2	0.2
Subtotal	7.9	5.2
+10% Waste	0.8	0.5
Total	8.7	5.7
MEF	Daily Gallons-Per-Man Requirements	
Function	Sustaining	Minimum
Drinking	3.0	3.0
Personal Hygiene	1.7	1.0
Field Feeding	2.8	0.8
Heat Casualty Treatment	0.2	0.2
Vehicle Maintenance	0.2	0.2
Level-1 Medical Treatment	0.4	0.4
Level-2 Medical Treatment	2.8	2.8
Centralized Hygiene	1.8	0.0
Construction	1.5	0.0
Aircraft Maintenance	0.2	0.2
Laundry	2.1	0.0
Subtotal	16.7	8.3
+10% Waste	1.7	0.9
Total	18.4	9.5

CHAPTER 11. WATER SUPPORT OPERATIONS

Effective water support is essential to mission accomplishment. The water support mission is to get potable water to each Marine. Each Service is responsible for its own water support. However, the Army is the theater manager for water support and may provide backup water support when the Services' requirements exceed their capabilities. When a Service requires backup water support, the supported Service must provide detailed water requirements to the Army planners. The Army will provide GS water support to other Services in the theater as required. FM 10-52 provides detailed information on Army roles and responsibilities for water support in the theater. The theater army material management command monitors water priorities and allocation procedures and provide the JTF commander with water supply data. During JTF operations, the JTF commander may assign water support responsibilities on an area basis. Under this "predominant user concept," the predominant Service in an area may be tasked to provide water support to all Services operating in that area above and beyond that Service's organic capabilities.

MAGTF Water Support Phases

MAGTFs may require water support for contingency operations in areas without a pre-established water support base to an operation involving allied/HN support. MAGTFs provide water support on an area basis using supply point distribution. Water support operations comprise three phases—water purification, water storage, and water distribution.

Water Purification

Water purification is the first phase of water support operations. During the purification phase, water is drawn from the source and purified to potable water standards. Potable water is certified safe for human consumption. Water is purified with a ROWPU, a medium freshwater purification unit, or the TWPS. Standards are verified by a member of an environmental protection medical unit or any corpsman with a water quality analysis kit and the knowledge of how to use it.

Water Storage

Water storage is the second phase of water support operations. Storage is normally done at or very close to the purification sites. The goal of water storage is to keep 1 DOS on hand. This will prevent a water shortage if several purification units go down simultaneously. Storage can be done using one (or a combination of) 500-gallon collapsible drum(s); SIXCON(s); 3,000-, 20,000-, and 50,000-gallon tanks.

Water Distribution

The third phase, water distribution, begins from the storage site. Water distribution is often the critical link in water support operations. If this link fails, the Marine goes thirsty. It is important that units organize so they will have sufficient organic water distribution equipment to provide supply point distribution. During the early phases of deployments and in emergency situations, packaged water will be the primary means of resupply in forward areas. As the CSSEs are established and LOCs are developed, units will begin pulling water from water points using organic 400-gallon water trailers and SIXCON water modules.

MAGTF Water Support Responsibilities

Normally the water supply system is an automatic resupply operation. Generally, its only limitations are water availability and the capability of receiving units. The forward movement of water is based on storage and distribution assets available.

MAGTF Command Element

The CE is responsible for overall water support planning and operations for the MAGTF. When demand exceeds supply, the MAGTF commander establishes an allocation system and support procedures. The allocation system is based on priorities to support the tactical plan.

To accomplish its mission, the CE performs the following tasks:

- Ensures water production, storage, and distribution is sufficient to support the entire MAGTF and any other water missions assigned by the JTF commander.
- Submits required water data to the JTF or theater Army.
- Directs storage and distribution procedures and priorities.
- Provides inventory management of GS water supplies and sets allocations if required.
- Ensures economy of management of all water support equipment within the MAGTF.

Other MAGTF Elements

The other elements of the MAGTF (GCE, ACE, and CSSE) are responsible for planning, directing, and supervising their organic water support assets. Each element will ensure it has the capabilities to perform any water support tasking assigned by the MAGTF commander. Daily management of the water points and water distribution is the responsibility of the GCE, ACE, and CSSE. Water support requirements that are beyond the organic capabilities of an element will be addressed to the MAGTF CE for sourcing. Each MAGTF element has water purification, distribution, and storage capability. However, the CSSE has the preponderance of water support equipment. As a result, the CSSE must be prepared to provide GS to the other elements of the MAGTF as needed.

Host Nation Considerations

HN water sources, facilities, and equipment should be used as much as possible. MAGTF water planners should assume that no HN water is available in arid regions. Minimal water sources and poor water quality may limit any operations that depend on HN support to meet the criteria set forth in NAVMED P-5010-5 or TB MED 577 for water quality standards. In the early stages of deployment, HN processed or bottled water may be used if preventive medicine personnel have certified it as potable. However, in both developed and undeveloped theaters, MAGTF commanders and water planners must be aware of the following regulations.

Water

Article 54 of the 1st Protocol to the Geneva Convention prohibits attacking, destroying, or rendering useless drinking water installations and supplies and irrigation works. In no event shall actions against these objects be taken which may be expected to leave the civilian population with such inadequate food or water as to cause its starvation or force its movement.

Refugees

Article 55 of the 4th Geneva Convention states that the host country, as the territorial sovereign, is responsible for refugees on its territory. In the event its resources are strained by an influx of refugees, the host country may request assistance from US forces. US forces would have a legal responsibility to provide refugee care where they have occupied enemy territory and have established a military government.

Enemy Prisoners of War

Article 26 of the 3d Geneva Convention requires the US to provide humane treatment to prisoners in its custody. This includes providing adequate water and food.

Labor Force Personnel

The HN is responsible for filling the needs of its labor forces unless otherwise provided in HNS agreements. In the absence of an agreement, US forces may have to assume some responsibility for the care of labor forces.

Regional Considerations

Arid Environment

Water sources are either nonexistent or extremely limited in arid regions. The options available to the MAGTF will be limited to importing water, desalinating seawater, or developing new water supply sources. Units will need to make maximum use of organic water equipment for storage and distribution. Water purification teams and detachments will often be required to operate from the shore purifying saltwater with ROWPUs. The family of water supply support equipment is used to store and distribute potable water to operating forces. Water moved forward is either stored in forward water supply points or issued to the using units. Water supply points are established as far forward as possible, considering the location of water sources, the location of using units, and the tactical plans. Based on resupply times and water availability, MAGTF commanders will have to establish the required DOS for water to be held at each echelon. Operational and DS units will normally maintain a minimum of 1 DOS.

Water supply operations in an arid environment are typically conducted in three phases to ensure effective and continual water support—development, lodgment, and buildup.

Development Phase

This phase may begin as an air or amphibious assault or as an uncontested entry at a friendly port. The first MAGTF elements will probably be combat forces with minimal CSS. Using canteens, 5-gallon cans, and other organic equipment, these forces carry only enough water for immediate survival purposes. Resupply must begin quickly by either air or from the sea. During this phase, packaged water will be primarily provided from offshore or from the air from nontheater support bases. Nonexpendable equipment used during this phase, such as 500-gallon drums and 5-gallon cans must be recovered and reused. MAGTF commanders must exploit all water sources while keeping the impact on the local population to a minimum.

Lodgment Phase

The arrival of follow-on forces in the AO will increase water requirements beyond the capabilities of aerial resupply except for forward deployed or isolated units. During this phase, in country water support systems must be established. CSS units will provide purification, storage, and distribution of water in support of the MAGTF. CSS units will exploit any source of water in the AO using organic water purification equipment.

Buildup Phase

Once the lodgment is established, expansion of the logistics base begins. Additional water support units and equipment will arrive. The distribution system should be expanded to include tactical water distribution system whenever possible. Bulk water can be introduced into the AOA via joint logistics over-the-shore. Water points will be expanded and moved as far forward as possible.

Nonarid Environment

Water support operations in an undeveloped, nonarid environment include development, lodgment, and buildup phases, and are identical to those described in the arid environment. There are three distinct nonarid environments or regions: temperate, tropical, and arctic. See chapter 10 for associated planning factors. Planning and operational considerations for each are discussed below:

Temperate Regions

Temperate regions have seasonal variations that may affect water support operations such as hot summers and cold winters. These variations may have a significant impact on where water points may be located. In spring and fall, heavy rains may flood streams and rivers. In the summer water sources may be low preventing sufficient water flow for purification operations. These factors require careful consideration by water planners and coordination with meteorology and map/area reconnaissance when selecting water sites.

Tropical Regions

Water sources in tropical regions are often contaminated with waterborne diseases and parasites. Although an abundance of water may be available in a tropical region, purification and treatment of raw water is required.

Arctic Regions

Water supply points in arctic regions must have equipment to prevent or retard freezing. Equipment can include shelters and heaters. Water sources in arctic regions will present unusual problems, including ground and source water freezing and distribution problems due to poor mobility.

APPENDIX A
PETROLEUM, OILS, AND LUBRICANTS APPENDIX TO THE LOGISTICS ANNEX

The following is the format for the petroleum, oils, and lubricants (POL) appendix for combatant commander, JTF, and MAGTF OPLANs and OPORDs.

CLASSIFICATION

Copy No. _____ of _____ copies
OFFICIAL DESIGNATION OF COMMAND
PLACE OF ISSUE
Date/time group
Message reference number

APPENDIX 1 TO ANNEX D TO OPLAN/PETROLEUM, OILS, AND LUBRICANTS SUPPLY (U)

(U) REFERENCES: [List documents necessary for a complete understanding of this appendix; include current petroleum studies, joint agreements, and other relevant guidance as applicable.]

1. (U) General

    a. (U) Purpose. State the purpose of this appendix.

    b. (U) Users. Describe the concept of petroleum supply operations by designating the users to be supported, including allied forces and civilian requirements, where applicable. Identify the agreements whereby support for the latter users would be undertaken.

2. (U) Concept of Operations

    a. (U) Availability and suitability of commercial petroleum products, petroleum storage, tanker unloading facilities, and petroleum distribution systems, within the AO.

    b. (U) Tanker offloading facilities and terminal facilities needed to meet US military requirements for petroleum support.

    c. (U) Concept of inland distribution.

    d. (U) Requirements for intertheater or intratheater movement of bulk petroleum to include points of origin, destination, type, and facilities available

CLASSIFICATION

CLASSIFICATION

or required to receive this type product. List POL data by product. Upon fielding of new time-phased force and deployment data format, the JOPES [Joint Operation Planning and Execution System] produced listing will be used.

e. (U) Requirement for local procurement of commercial petroleum products and petroleum distribution and storage services within the AO.

f. (U) Establishment of a quality control activity within the AO.

3. (U) <u>Responsibilities</u>

a. (U) Assign specific tasks to military organizations, including the component commanders, when appropriate.

b. (U) Delineate support responsibilities of the joint petroleum office, JTF, JTF component commanders, subarea petroleum offices, appropriate unified commands or their components, for the supply of petroleum, including responsibility for its transportation.

4. (U) <u>Limiting Factors</u>. Describe limitations that could adversely affect petroleum supply operations, such as inadequate air and ocean terminal capacity, lack of storage facilities, malpositioned storage, inadequate transportation, inadequate in-theater stocks, lack of alternate facilities, and similar logistic constraints.

5. (U) <u>Estimate of POL Support Requirements</u>. Refer to TAB A, if applicable. Describe methodology used to compute requirements if Service planning factors were not applicable or if unique factors were considered.

ACKNOWLEDGE RECEIPT

> Name
> Rank and Service
> Title

Page number

CLASSIFICATION

APPENDIX B
PETROLEUM ALLOCATION
DEFENSE MESSAGE SYSTEM

The following is a message text format report that is used to identify bulk petroleum allocations (POLALOTs) when required. The report may be used by the combatant commander to the component commands and by the MEF to the major subordinate commands. The report is only used when bulk petroleum stocks or support cannot meet all the requirements. For instructions and codes, refer to the defense message system.

Bulk Petroleum Allocation
POLALOT

```
FM JTF/COMMARFOR
TO II MEF
CG MAW//G4/G3//
CG MARDIV//G4/G3//
CG FSSG//G3/G4//
CC (AS REQUIRED)
BT UNCLAS//N04020//
EXER//OPER//
MSGID/POLALOT/MEF G4/0001/NOV//
REF//
AMPN//
NARR//
PERID/150500Z/TO:160500Z/ASOF:141800Z//
6POL /
CMPCMD          /FUELTYP/QTY /UOVOLM/POLDELMD/DELPOS /
MAW             /JP5     /100K/GAL /TKRTRK /LZ BLUEBIRD /
MAW             /MUR     / 5K/GAL /TKRTRK /LZ BLUEBIRD /
FSSG            /DF2     / 20K/GAL /BARGE /LZ BLUEDIRD /
FSSG            /MUR     / 10K/GAL /TKRTRK /LZ FALCON /
FSSG            /JP8     / 50K/GAL /TKRTRK /LZ FALCON /
FSSG            /JP5     /600K/GAL /TKRSHP /ONSLOW BEACH /
MARDIV          /DF2     / 25K/GAL /TKRTRK /GRID 432756 /
MARDIV          /DF2     / 5K/GAL /TKRAC /GRID 479832//
BT #
```

APPENDIX C
BULK PETROLEUM CONTINGENCY REPORT
MESSAGE TEXT FORMAT REPORT

The following is a message text format report that is used to provide summary information on bulk fuel inventories, damage, and damage assessment on bulk fuel distribution systems. The REPOL is normally submitted by the combatant commander, joint petroleum office or subarea petroleum office. The MEF will submit REPOL feeder reports as required by the combatant commander to the appropriate agency.

Bulk Petroleum Contingency Report

SECRET when filled out (insert date here)

A	B	C	D	E
PART I				
LOCATION				
(insert town or city and <u>grid)</u>				
	ISSUED	RECEIPTS	ON-HAND	STORAGE
PRODUCT	LAST 24 HOURS	LAST 24 HOURS	INVENTORY	CAPACITY
JP-8	X	X	X	X
AVGAS	X	X	X	X
MOGAS	X	X	X	X
PART II Forecast				
	24 HOURS	48 HOURS	72 HOURS	96 HOURS
JP-8	X	X	X	X
AVGAS	X	X	X	X
MOGAS	X	X	X	X
PART III Equipment				
				STORAGE
TYPE SYSTEM (capacity)	ON HAND	IN-SERVICE	NOTES	PER
AAFS (1.2 million)	X	X		1,200,000
TAFDS (320K)	X	X		320,000
TAFDS (120K)	X	X		120,000
HERS (9K/18K)	X	X		9,000/18,000
ARC (5K)	X	X		5,000
M970	X	X		5,000
PART IV Personnel				
	ON HAND			
Enlisted Petroleum Supply Spec	X			
M970 Driver/mechanic	X			
Petroleum Officer	X			
PART V Remarks				
Prepared by: Rank and name	XXXXXXXX			
Telephone #: valid/accurate telephone#	XXXXXXXX			

APPENDIX D. GLOSSARY

PART I. ACRONYMS AND ABBREVIATIONS

AABFS . . . . .amphibious assault bulk fuel system (Navy)
AAFS . . . . amphibious assault fuel system (USMC)
ACE . . . . aviation combat element
ALOC . . . . .air line of communications
AMC . . . . Air Mobility Command
AO . . . . .area of operations
AOA . . . . amphibious objective area
API . . . . American Petroleum Institute
ARC . . . . aviation refueling capability
ASTM . . . . .American Society for Testing and Materials
AVGAS. . . . . aviation gasoline

BTU . . . . British thermal unit

C . . . . Celsius
CE . . . . command element
COMMZ . . . . .communications zone
CONUS. . . . . continental United States
CSS . . . . combat service support
CSSD . . . . combat service support detachment
CSSE . . . . .combat service support element
cSt . . . . .centistoke

DESC . . . . .Defense Energy Support Center
DOD . . . . Department of Defense
DODD. . . . . . . Department of Defense directive
DOS . . . . day(s) of supply
DS . . . . direct support

ERS . . . . expedient refueling system
ESB . . . . engineer support battalion

F . . . . Fahrenheit
FARP . . . . forward arming and refueling point
FAWPSS. . . . . forward area water point supply system
FM. . . . . field manual
FSII . . . . fuel system icing inhibitor
FSSG . . . . force service support group
FW . . . . fixed wing

G-3 . . . . Army or Marine Corps component operations staff officer (Army division or higher staff, Marine Corps brigade or higher staff)
G-4 . . . . Army or Marine Corps component logistics staff officer (Army division or higher staff, Marine Corps brigade or higher staff)
gal . . . . gallon(s)
GCE . . . . ground combat element
GPH . . . . gallons per hour
GPM . . . . gallons per minute
GS . . . . .general support

HERS . . . . .helicopter expedient refueling system
HN. . . . . host nation
HNS . . . . .host-nation support

IMP . . . . .inventory management plan
IPDS . . . . .inland petroleum distribution system (Army)
ISO . . . . International Organization for Standardization

J-4 . . . . .logistics directorate of a joint staff; logistics staff section
JFC . . . . .joint force commander
JOPES . . . . .Joint Operation Planning and Execution System
JPO . . . . .joint petroleum office
JTF . . . . joint task force

K . . . . .thousand

lb . . . . .pound(s)
LOC . . . . lines of communication

MAGTF . . . . Marine air-ground task force
MARDIV . . . . Marine division
MARFOR . . . . .Marine Corps forces
MAW . . . . .Marine aircraft wing
MCWP . . .Marine Corps warfighting publication
MEB . . . . Marine expeditionary brigade

MEF . . . . Marine expeditionary force
MEU . . . . Marine expeditionary unit
MIL-DTL . . . . military detail specification
MIL-STD . . . . military standard
MOGAS . . . . motor gasoline
MOS . . . . military occupational specialty
MPS . . . . maritime prepositioning ship
MPSRON . . . . maritime prepositioning
ships squadron
MWSG . . . . Marine wing support group
MWSS . . . . Marine wing support squadron

NATO . . . . . . North Atlantic Treaty Organization
NAVAIR . . . . Naval Air Systems Command
NAVMED . . . . Navy Medical Command
NBC . . . . nuclear, biological, and
chemical
NOLSC . . . . Naval Operational Logistics
Support Center
NSN . . . . National Stock Number

OPDS . . . . offshore petroleum discharge
system (Navy)
OPLAN . . . . operation plan
POL . . . . petroleum, oils, and lubricants
POLALOT . . . . petroleum allocation
psi . . . . pounds per square inch
PWRR . . . . . petroleum war reserve requirement
PWRS . . . . petroleum war reserve stocks

REPOL . . . . bulk petroleum
contingency report
ROWPU . . . . reverse osmosis water
purification unit
RW . . . . rotary wing

S-3 . . . . battalion or brigade operations
staff officer (Army;
Marine Corps battalion
or regiment)
S-4 . . . . battalion or brigade logistics
staff officer (Army;
Marine Corps battalion
or regiment)
SAPO . . . . subarea petroleum office
SIPRNET . . . . Secret Internet Protocol
Router Network
SIXCON . . . . six containers together
SOA . . . . sustained operations ashore
SOP . . . . standing operating procedure
STS . . . . ship to shore

TAFDS . . . . tactical airfield fuel
dispensing system
TAMCN . . . . table of authorized materiel
control number
TBFDS . . . . tactical bulk fuel
distribution system
TB MED . . . . technical bulletin, medical
TFS . . . . tactical fuel systems
TPLM . . . . tactical petroleum laboratory,
medium
TWDS . . . . tactical water distribution system
TWPS . . . . tactical water purification system

US . . . . United States
USAPC . . . . US Army Petroleum Center
USMC . . . . United States Marine Corps

WQAS-P . . . . water quality analysis
set-purification
WSSE . . . . water supply support equipment

PART II. DEFINITIONS

additive—An agent used for improving existing characteristics or for giving new characteristics to certain petroleum products. (FM 10-67)

aerial refueling—The use of aerial tanker-configured aircraft to provide refueling service to helicopters, fixed-wing, and tilt-rotor aircraft in flight. Aerial refueling extends the range, time on station, mobility, and flexibility of MAGTF aircraft. (MCRP 5-12C)

American Petroleum Institute—The institute represents and is supported by the petroleum industry. It standardizes the tools and equipment used by the industry and promotes the advancement of research in the petroleum field. Also called **API**. (FM 10-67-1)

American Society for Testing and Materials—A national scientific and technical organization formed for the development of standards or characteristics and performance of materials, products, systems, and services and the promotion of related knowledge. Also called **ASTM**.

amphibious assault bulk fuel system—The US Navy system of flexible, buoyant hose used to effect ship-to-shore transfer of fuels. Five thousand feet of 6-inch hose connects amphibious shipping to shorebased fuel storage systems located at the high water mark. Also called **AABFS**. (MCRP 5-12C)

amphibious assault fuel system—The Marine Corps' primary fuel storage system used to support amphibious operations. This system is composed of a number of components capable of receiving, transferring, and dispensing motor gasoline, diesel, or aviation fuels. The system can be set up in a wide variety of configurations to meet varying operational requirements. Also called **AAFS**. (MCRP 5-12C)

amphibious objective area—A geographical area (delineated for command and control purposes in the order initiating the amphibious operation) within which is located the objective(s) to be secured by the amphibious force. This area must be of sufficient size to ensure accomplishment of the amphibious force's mission and must provide sufficient area for conducting necessary sea, air, and land operations. Also called **AOA**. (JP 1-02)

API gravity—An arbitrary scale expressing the gravity or density of liquid petroleum products. The measuring scale is calibrated in terms of degrees API. The gravity of any petroleum product is corrected to 60 degrees F (16 degrees C). (FM 10-67-1)

appearance—Refers to the visual examination of fuels. The terms used to describe appearance are clear and bright, hazy and cloudy. (FM 10-67-1)

barrel—A common unit of measurement of liquids in the petroleum industry. It equals 42 US standard gallons. (FM 10-67)

berm—An earthen wall constructed around a fuel tank to contain potential fuel leaks or spills.

berm liner—A cloth or plastic tarp, impervious to fuel, used to line a berm.

blending—Mixing on-specification fuel with off specification fuel to bring the latter to specification or use limits. Used as a method of reclamation.

bonding—Making an electrical connection between items of equipment/tanks. Bonding equalizes electrical potential between items, and reduces the threat of sparks due to static electricity passing between the items of equipment.

bottom sediment and water—Amount of sediment and water in the bottom of fuel tanks.

bulk fuel company—A unit that performs all functions incident to the supply of class III and class III(A) to elements of a MAGTF, to include distribution to, but not within, air bases during an amphibious assault and subsequent operations ashore; to ensure that class III(A) products distributed to supported air elements are of the required type, quality, and purity. (MCRP 5-12C)

bulk liquid—Fuel or water itself, not inclusive of the container or handling apparatus. A term also used to define quantities of fuel or water above either 55 gallons or 250/500 gallons; the former when handling product in 55-gallon metal drums is common, the latter when 250/500-gallon collapsible water drums or 500-gallon collapsible fuel drums are in use.

bulk petroleum products—Those petroleum products (fuels, lubricants) which are normally transported by pipeline, rail tank car, tank truck, barge, or tanker and stored in tanks or containers having a capacity of more than 55 gallons, except fuels in 500-gallon collapsible containers, which are considered to be packaged. (FM 10-67)

carbon dioxide—A heavy, colorless gas, CO2, that will not support combustion (therefore, useful as a fire-extinguishing agent). (FM 10-67-1)

carbon monoxide—A colorless, odorless, and poisonous gas, CO, resulting from the incomplete combustion of carbon. (FM 10-67-1)

centrifuge—A whirling instrument for separating liquids or liquids and solids of different specific gravity by use of centrifugal force. (FM 10-67)

Class III—Petroleum products; petroleum, oils and lubricants often broken down into Class IIIA for aviation fuel, and Class III(W) for ground equipment fuel.

combat service support detachment—A separate task organization of combat service support assets formed for the purpose of providing rearming, refueling, and/or repair capabilities to the Marine air-ground task force or designated subordinate elements; e.g., a battalion conducting independent operations or an aircraft squadron operating at a remote airfield. The combat service support element normally provides the command element of a combat service support detachment. Also called **CSSD**. (MCRP 5-12C)

contaminant—A foreign substance in a product. (FM 10-67-1)

Defense Energy Support Center—An activity under the Defense Logistics Agency with the responsibility as the integrated material manager

for wholesale bulk petroleum products until their delivery to the point of sale. This responsibility includes contract administration in an oversee area. Also called **DESC**. (FM 10-70-1)

defense fuel supply point—Any military or commercial bulk fuel terminal storing products owned by the Defense Logistics Agency. Also called **DFSP**. (FM 10-67-1)

Defense Logistics Agency—The agency, at the Department of Defense level, charged with providing the most effective and economical support of common supplies and services to the Military Departments and other designated Department of Defense components. It is the agency under which Defense Energy Support Center operates. Also called **DLA**. (FM 10-67-1)

drum—Either 16- or 18-gage steel cylindrical containers (generally, 55-gallon size) or 250/500-gallon collapsible water containers/500-gallon collapsible fuel containers.

flashpoint—The temperature at which a fuel will "flash" when exposed to test flame flame diameter of approximately 1/8 inch, like a butane lighter flame adjusted as low as possible; also a test performed per the American Society for Testing and Materials.

force service support group—The combat service support element of the Marine expeditionary force. It is a permanently organized Fleet Marine Force command charged with providing combat service support beyond the organic capabilities of supported units of the Marine expeditionary force. If supporting a force of greater size, additional assets are necessary to augment its capabilities. Although permanently structured with eight functional battalions, task organizations from those battalions would normally support Marine expeditionary force operations over a wide geographic area. Also called **FSSG**. (MCRP 5-12C)

forward arming and refueling point—A temporary facility—organized, equipped, and deployed by an aviation commander, and normally located in the main battle area closer to the area of operation than the aviation unit's combat service area—to provide fuel and ammunition necessary for the employment of aviation maneuver units in combat. The forward arming and refueling point permits combat aircraft to rapidly refuel and rearm simultaneously. Also called **FARP**. (JP 1-02)

gallon—A unit of measure of volume. A US gallon contains 231 cubic inches or 3.785 liters; it is 0.83268 times the imperial gallon. One US gallon of water weighs 8.3374 pounds at 60 degrees F (16 degrees C). (FM 10-67-1)

ground cloth—A protective cloth placed beneath collapsible bulk liquid tanks to protect the bottom of the tank from sharp objects.

grounding—Electrically connecting single or bonded units to a ground rod so static potential is discharged into the earth.

halon—Halogenated hydrocarbon fuel fire extinguishing agent. It comes in various chemical composition models; Halon 1211, Halon 1301, etc.

inventory—Bulk tankage contents measured to current product level; includes tank bottoms and associated pipeline fill. (FM 10-67-1)

joint petroleum office—An office established by the Joint Chiefs of Staff with petroleum logistics responsibilities in a unified command in overseas areas. (FM 10-67-1)

petroleum—Crude oil. Petroleum is a mixture of gaseous, liquid, and semisolids hydrocarbons varying widely in gravity and complexity. Petroleum can be removed as a liquid from underground reservoirs, and it can be separated into various fractions by distillation and recovery. Petroleum is a general term that includes all petroleum fuels, lubricants, and specialties. (FM 10-67-1)

rear operations—Military actions conducted to support and permit force sustainment and to provide security for such actions. (MCRP 5-12C)

reverse osmosis—The application of pressure to a concentrated solution which causes the passage of a liquid from the concentrated solution to a weaker solution across a semipermeable membrane. The membrane allows the passage of the solvent (water) but not the dissolved solids (solutes). The liquid produced is a demineralized water. (FM 10-70-1; FM 10-52)

sortie—In air operations, an operational flight by one aircraft. (JP 1-02)

specification—Prescribed limits of control tests used to maintain uniformity of a specific product. (FM 10-67-1)

storage capacity—Total of existing bulk tankage assigned for product storage. Capacity is measured to maximum fill level for each tank and includes nonrecoverable tank bottoms. (FM 10-67-1)

subarea petroleum office—A sub-office of a JPO established by the JPO to fulfill petroleum logistics responsibilities in a section of the geographical area for which the JPO is responsible. Also called **SAPO**. (FM 10-67-1)

tactical airfield fuel dispensing system—An expeditionary system providing bulk fuel storage and dispensing facilities at airfields not having permanently installed fuel systems; also used to support fuel dispensing at established airfields. Also called **TAFDS**. (MCRP 5-12C)

tank—A storage container for liquid products.

tanker—A seagoing vessel for transporting liquids. Coastal tankers have less draft (depth of a ship below the waterline) than oceangoing tankers. (FM 10-67-1) terminal—A bulk facility for receipt, storage, transportation, and issue of petroleum products. The facility may be a *base terminal* for receipt and shipment of product by tanker, a *pipehead terminal (head terminal)* at the downstream end of the pipeline, or an *intermediate terminal* on the pipeline. The terminal consists of a tank farm or tank farm complex, tank farm manifold, and central pump station area. (FM 10-67-1)

total dissolved solids—All of the dissolved solids in a water. Total dissolved solids are measured on a sample of water that has passed through a very fine mesh filter to remove suspended solids. The water passing through the filter evaporated and the residue represents the dissolved solids. (FM 10-52)

ullage—The amount by which a container, storage tank, or storage facility falls short of being full.

volume correction—The correction of measured quantity of product, determined by gauging at observed temperature and gravity and reference to a gage table, to net quantity of product at 60 degrees F (16 degrees C) after deducting bottom water and sediment. (FM 10-67-1)

water—An odorless, colorless, transparent liquid, solid (ice), or gas (steam), compound H_2O.

water, dissolved—All fuel contains some water in solution, and amounts will vary with temperature. This type water is not separated from fuel by filter separators or other mechanical means.

water, entrained—"Free" water which is suspended throughout a fuel (or sample) and has not yet settled to the bottom of fuel container/tank.

APPENDIX E. REFERENCES

Department of Defense Directives (DODDs)

4140.25	DOD Management Policy for Energy Commodities and Related Services
5101.8	DOD Executive Agent (EA) for Bulk Petroleum

Department of Defense Military Specification (MILSPEC)

DTL-5624T	Turbine Fuel, Aviation, Grades JP-4 and JP-5
DTL-83133E	Turbine Fuel, Aviation, Grade JP-8
G-5572	Gasoline, Aviation, Grades 80/87, 100/130, 115/145
A-A-52557	Fuel oil, Diesel; for Posts, Camps and Stations
MIL-F-16884	Fuel, Navy Distillate

Chairman of the Joint Chiefs of Staff Manual (CJCSM)

3122.03A	Joint Operation Planning and Execution System (JOPES), Volume II, Planning Formats and Guidance

Department of Defense Military Standard (MIL-STD)

3004-A	Quality Surveillance for Fuels, Lubricants, and Related Products

Department of Defense (DOD) Publication

4140.25-M	DOD Management of Bulk Petroleum Products, Natural Gas, and Coal (Volumes I-IV)
4715.5G	Overseas Environmental Baseline Guidance Document

Joint Publication (JP)

4-03	Joint Bulk Petroleum and Water Doctrine

Naval Air Systems Command (NAVAIR) Publication

00-80T-109	Aircraft Refueling Naval Air Training and Operating Procedures Standardization (NATOPS) Manual

Navy Medical Command (NAVMED) Publication

P-5010-5   Preventive Medicine Manual (Chapter 5, Water
                                              Supply Ashore)

Marine Corps Doctrinal Publication (MCDP)

4   Logistics

Marine Corps Warfighting Publications (MCWPs)

3-17   Engineer Operations
4-1   Logistics Operations
4-11.7   MAGTF Supply Operations

Marine Corps Order (MCO)

P5090.2A   Environmental Compliance and Protection
                                              Manual

Air Force Technical Order (AF TO)

42   Security System Data

Army Field Manuals (FMs)

10-52   Water Supply in Theaters of Operations
10-52-1   Water Supply Point Equipment and Operations

Army Technical Bulletin, Medical (TB MED)

577   Occupational and Environmental Health:
                                              Sanitary Control and Surveillance of
                                              Field Water Supplies

American Society for Testing and Materials (ASTM) Specifications

D-3240-91 (2001)   Standard Test Method for Undissolved Water
                                              in Aviation Turbine Fuels

D-1655-04   Standard Specification for Aviation
                                              Turbine Fuels

D-4814   Standard Specifications for Automotive Spark-
                                              Ignition Engine Fuel